D0525852

TAKE ONE POT

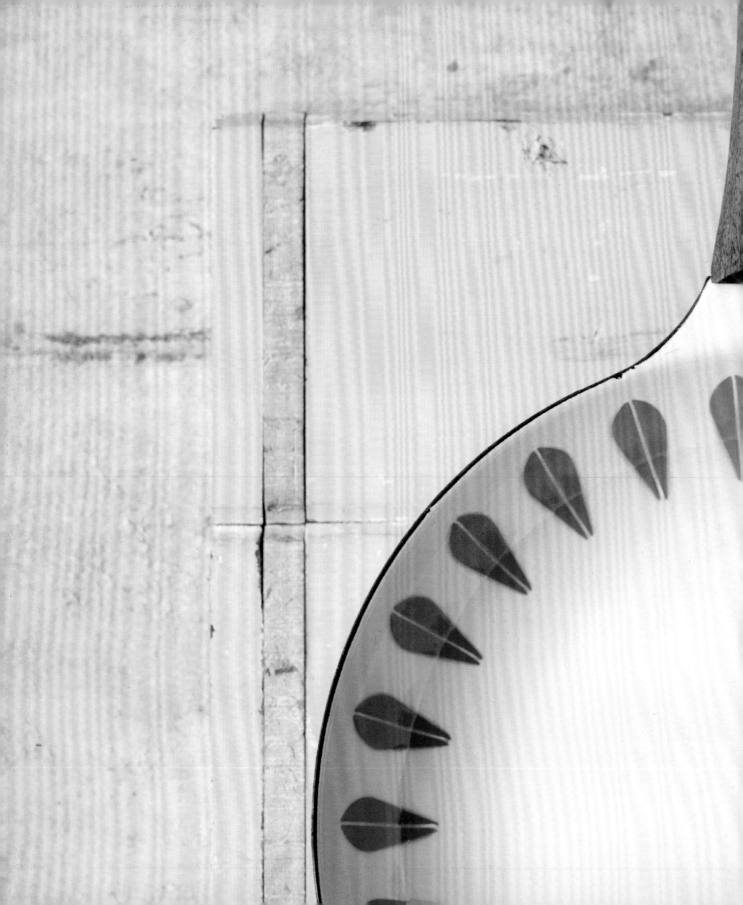

TAKE ONE POT

Super simple recipes to cook
in one pot, full stop

GEORGINA FUGGLE

....

Photography by

Tara Fisher

KYLE BOOKS

Published in Great Britain in 2013 by
Kyle Books
23 Howland Street
London W1T 4AY
www.kylebooks.com

ISBN: 978 085783 070 8

10 9 8 7 6 5 4 3 2 1

Photography: Tara Fisher
Design: Nicky Collings
Prop styling: Wei Tang
Food styling: Georgina Fuggle and Joss Herd
Project editor: Sophie Allen
Copy editor: Emily Hatchwell
Production: Gemma John and Nic Jones

A CIP record for this title is available from the British Library.

Colour reproduction by Scanhouse
Printed and bound in China by C&C Offset Printing Co. Ltd

Thank you to Le Creuset and Staub for lending us their wonderful pots.

ACKNOWLEDGEMENTS

I've had quite a clear list of children's names in my mind for some years now and it's a funny thing when you discover one has been stolen from you. Sophie, the most wonderful editor, had already named her beautiful boy with the name at the very top of my list, but I still couldn't help liking her. Thank you for gently steering me, Tuesday night suppers and walking me to the bus stop. May there be many more conversations and lots more laughter.

Tara and Nicky have been instrumental – just imagine this book with no pictures and no clever design. It's been gorgeous to spend days shooting in Brixton together, eating a few more pecan Danishes than were really necessary.

Alice. You are a perfect friend and a real inspiration to me. Who else would think to send a birthday cake decorated with zero when I announced my pregnancy? I've loved all the things we've done together and look forward to future antics.

Hannah. You've tested and retested with the most infectious enthusiasm. I'm so grateful to you. And Sarah, I couldn't have hoped for a better assistant.

Oenone and Will have eaten far more than their fair share of one pots throughout swelteringly hot summer days and helped me re-work and re-test recipes until we all felt pleased. My lovely mother-in-law, Sue, has cooked any recipes I felt needed a second opinion and frequently made inconvenient changes to schedules to squeeze in a one pot. Far beyond the call of duty but very, very much appreciated.

It's quite humbling to think how many people have steered me along this path, but there is one in particular who deserves a very public thank you. My Mumma has eaten little else but one pot meals, she has driven all over north Norfolk in search of fresh dill and learnt to enjoy a pig cheek or two. She has always said my pots are delicious. She has always gone above and beyond. Thank you.

Julia, Rachel, Henrietta, Annabel and Rosie tested and fed their families with the results! I hope they were happy. You are all heroes.

And Nicko. You are endlessly encouraging and the person I would like most to share my table with. You are the Fuggle to my heart.

CONTENTS

ONE POT, FULL STOP.

My mind takes a few minutes to rouse in the morning. If I'm good I wake and say a quick prayer before deciding what to eat for breakfast. If I'm bad I just decide what I can eat for breakfast. Talking, writing and tasting food is how many of my hours are spent and still I delight in cooking like an enthusiastic honeybee.

The delight began when I was just a girl; a car boot sale had been advertised, two weeks on Saturday in the village hall car park. Others scrabbled around their bedrooms gathering treasure while I buzzed around the kitchen baking plump cheese straws and currant scones. Our wares were bagged up, each costing but a few pennies, and we set sail for the elusive stall. I remember our profit being just a few pounds, but to me, an impressionable 12-year-old, this was the launch into professional cooking that I so desperately wanted.

Years passed, cooking methods were explored and preferences formed, but it was a Christmas present of a chrome black Le Creuset that ignited fervour for the one pot. Home was a miniscule flat in Waterloo where there was absolutely no space for a food processor or a microwave. A sink, an oven, a tiny utensils drawer and my huge black pot made up the bulk of a very cherished kitchen.

Practice makes perfect, we've all been told, and practise I did. Inspired by the classics but pushed forward by a London food scene bursting on my doorstep, I cooked long into the night. It was quite usual to be woken by the buzz of an alarm clock disturbing sleep to turn off a simmering stew. Then I would sneak back to bed, choosing to ignore the water, heat, steam, fury and grease all over my beloved ktichen.

May I present to you my findings, my scrapbook of beloved one pots, each of which has been tasted and tested and has triumphed on the table. Each of which I hope will make you happy.

A FEW TIPS THAT I'VE LEARNT ALONG THE WAY

Sharp Knives

These are actually far safer to use than their blunt cousins; they glide through ingredients rather than needing to be forced with excess pressure, so reduce emergency trips to locate plasters (or even your nearest A & E). Ask your local butcher to help keep your set sharp – most of them will happily oblige.

Brown Your Meat Thoroughly

Few cooks realise how long it takes to brown meat thoroughly but the process is, in my opinion, the most important stage of stews. Be patient; control the heat as best you can. A good rule of thumb is: if it's brown, flavour has developed; if it's black, the pot is in danger of tasting a little bitter.

Oven Thermometer

Years of being a food editor taught me that ovens have different responses to being told to preheat to certain temperatures. A thermometer is worth its weight in gold when you're following a recipe, particularly one that involves a dish that sits in the oven for a good few hours.

Preparation, Preparation, Preparation

Most stews benefit from a day or two just sitting, getting to know themselves a little better. If you have friends coming over, make the stew in advance so you have less to do on the day. Both the chef and the pot will be more content.

Liquids

I learnt that anything is better than water in a stew. Don't throw away bottles of anything. If the wine is too dismal to be drunk at the table, it can be used to cut through oil for a salad dressing or top up stock in a recipe. For stock, use the tiny cubes if you have to, but most supermarkets stock a more upmarket version in the form of pouches. If you haven't time to make homemade stock, these are your best bet.

Don't Rush

Most of my pots simmer at a low temperature for a little longer than it might take to pick up a sandwich at Starbucks, but they are worth the wait. Allow the meat to grow tender in its own time; if it's not falling apart, sit back and have another glass of wine while you wait.

The All Important Pot

I'm not a food snob, I promise. There has been many a happy occasion when a good takeaway or dirty kebab has been coveted and, let's face it, enjoyed. However, I do, occasionally, raise my nose at people's cooking pots. Pasta, potatoes, rice, noodles – anything you can think of – enjoys having some room to boil. Always use a size bigger than you think is needed.

A heavy, iron-based pot will make your life easier as you can fry and stew in the very same one and it means less washing up, so smiles all round!

What to Stock Up On

There is little more satisfying than conjuring a fabulous meal from your very own store cupboard. Avoiding any trawl to the shops makes me feel like I've achieved, ticked the 'organised mother' bracket and my ego can be indulged with a proverbial pat on the back. But alas, too often, my store cupboards have let me down at the critical, post-work, hypoglycaemic moment when babies are screaming and a friend has just called to confirm that 'dinner is on?'

So, what should those dreaded cupboards contain to help you along the one-pot highway?

Maldon Sea Salt – The crunch is glorious and the flavour intensifies any stew, soup or chocolate pot. As much as salt shakers have their purpose, very rarely do they do the job as quickly or efficiently as a healthy hand pinch from a box of Maldon.

Tinned Italian Chopped Tomatoes – Yes, one is able to buy cheap, watery tomatoes but if your recipe requires just one tin, and the tomatoes should actually be tasted, then do invest in your store cupboard and stock up on some good-quality tinned tomatoes. I can't tell you exactly when they will rescue you during a culinary breakdown, but they will, I'm sure of it.

Olive oil – There are certainly moments for vegetable oil among recipes but equally there are times when your ingredients deserve to be coated in gold. Extra virgin olive oil is indeed worth the expense, especially when it's the final drizzle over a dish before it reaches the table.

Onions – The backbone to a stew, onions need to be treated with the utmost respect. Occasionally I have asked for them to be flash fried, thrown into boiling oil until their edges curl, but more often they should be gently, sympathetically cooked over a lower heat for a few more minutes.

Dark Brown Sugar – It's both the caramel brown colour and the complex caramel taste that pushes me to use just a touch of brown sugar in savoury recipes. Often it can take the edge off a bitter onion or tart alcoholic taste.

MOTHER SOUPERIA

As a bishop's daughter, the title of this particular chapter resonates with my home-grown self. I think sitting amongst pews in a church nourishes the soul in a similar way to a hearty bowl of soup.

The recipes are simple; the pots generally look after themselves. The fine line between a soup and a stew is very nearly crossed in a number of the following recipes, but a chunky soup can be exactly what is needed following a gruelling day at work or a bracing winter walk. Equally, an elegant beetroot number can kick-start a dinner party in an oh-so-sophisticated fashion.

The choice is yours.

BEETROOT & ORANGE SOUP
WITH SOUR CREAM

This dish is one of my favourites, developing the humble, earth-dwelling beetroot into a recipe fit for a king, with velvety texture, complexity of flavours, not to mention regal purple colour. These majestic features are enhanced by an acidic splash of orange and a smooth scoop of sour cream which completes the transformation from rags to riches.

PREP TIME 15 MINUTES   SERVES 6   COOK TIME 1.5 HOURS

1 tablespoon vegetable oil

2 red onions, roughly chopped

3 huge garlic cloves, peeled and finely sliced

2 sticks of celery, roughly chopped

½ teaspoon ground cinnamon

500g beetroot, peeled and cut into 1–2cm cubes

1.2 litre hot vegetable stock

Grated zest and juice of 1 large orange

Sea salt and freshly ground black pepper

6 spoonfuls of sour cream, to serve

1 Heat the vegetable oil in the bottom of a large saucepan and add the onions, garlic and celery. Cook, covered, on a very very gentle heat for 15 minutes, until the vegetables are soft and panting from exhaustion; add the cinnamon for the final 5 minutes. Stir every so often to make sure nothing is turning to coal.

2 Add the cubed beetroot to the pot and cook for 5–10 minutes until it begins to soften. Pour over the stock, season well, then cover and simmer for 1 hour or until the beetroot is tender and cuts like butter.

3 Use a stick blender or food processor to whiz the soup in batches until smooth. Try to avoid turning your kitchen purple! Return the soup to the saucepan and stir through the fresh orange juice. Anoint with cold sour cream and a sprinkling of orange zest before serving.

LEEK, KALE
& BARLEY BROTH

Cheap food can be beautiful food and this is a fine example of that. Pearl barley has a nutty, unassuming sort of taste and is a perfect 'filler' in an autumnal soup like this one. I've cooked it in chicken stock as I think it has a slightly punchier flavour, but of course you could switch to vegetable stock and make it tee-total vegetarian.

PREP TIME 15 MINUTES   MAKES 6–8 MUGFULS   COOK TIME 50 MINUTES

2 tablespoons olive oil

2 medium leeks, finely sliced

4 garlic cloves, peeled and sliced

3 sprigs of thyme

100g pearl barley

2 litres hot chicken stock

200g curly kale, stems removed, washed thoroughly
   and roughly chopped

2 tablespoons roughly chopped flat-leaf parsley

Sea salt and freshly ground black pepper

FOR THE SALTED PAPRIKA YOGURT

200g crème fraîche

Grated zest of 1 lemon and juice of ½ lemon

½ teaspoon Spanish smoked paprika

2 good pinches of salt

1 Heat the olive oil in a large, deep saucepan. Add the leeks and garlic and cook over a medium heat for 2–3 minutes until the leeks have begun to turn translucent, but don't allow them to colour.

2 Add the sprigs of thyme and season well. Cover and continue to cook on a very low heat for 10 minutes until the leeks have wilted, stirring occasionally to stop anything catching on the bottom of the pan. Stir the pearl barley into the pot and pour over the hot chicken stock. Simmer gently for 30–40 minutes until the barley is tender.

3 Stir in the kale towards the end of the cooking time, allowing it to boil for 6–8 minutes. Top up with a little more hot stock if you think it's needed. It's lovely for the kale to retain some of its crunch and vibrant green, so don't cook it for longer than needed.

4 For the salted paprika yogurt, simply combine the crème fraîche, lemon zest, juice, paprika and salt and allow to sit while the soup develops.

5 Ladle into the mugs and serve your soup with parsley bobbing in it and a good heap of paprika yogurt.

POTATO, PROSCIUTTO

& ROSEMARY SOUP

There is a fine line between a chunky soup and a light stew and this recipe could fall into either camp. Very simple ingredients create a frugal soup that pretty much takes care of itself. Just drop everything in and let the saucepan do the hard work.

PREP TIME 10 MINUTES   SERVES 6   COOK TIME 35 MINUTES

3 tablespoons butter (or 50g)

1 large onion, peeled and roughly chopped

½ tablespoon finely chopped rosemary

550g floury potatoes, peeled and cut into 2cm dice

800ml hot chicken stock

200ml milk

6 slices of prosciutto, torn into slithers

A little cream, to finish

Sea salt and freshly ground black pepper

1 Melt the butter in a heavy-bottomed saucepan over a medium heat. Reduce the heat to low and add the onion, rosemary and potato chunks, stirring gently. Season well, cover with a lid and allow the vegetables to soften for about 12 minutes without colouring. Give the saucepan a good shake half way through to prevent anything catching on the bottom.

2 Add the stock and milk to the pan, stir thoroughly and continue to cook for a further 20 minutes or until the potatoes are falling apart. Purée the soup in a blender or using a stick blender.

3 Give the soup a good taste to make sure the seasoning is correct and serve with slithers of prosciutto and cream balancing on the surface.

FISH SOUP

WITH A TOUCH OF THE EAST

Nothing prepares an English girl for the perils of Thai backstreets. Incessant hooting, oppressive heat and street vendor carts showcasing Pad Thai and deep-fried crabs paint a vivid picture of a vibrant country. I remember the smell of fresh lime and coriander bouncing from pots and brothy noodles being slurped by the locals. This fish soup reminds me of those warm days and can be a welcome escape from bleak British weather.

PREP TIME 15 MINUTES   SERVES 4   COOK TIME 30 MINUTES

1 teaspoon sunflower oil

2 garlic cloves, peeled and diced

1.2 litres fish stock

2 small bird's eye chillies, finely chopped

2 lemongrass stems, bruised and cut in half lengthways

A few fresh coriander stalks, finely chopped

5cm piece of fresh ginger, peeled and finely chopped

400ml coconut milk

300g raw king prawns, peeled and deveined but with tails still attached

250g salmon fillet, cut into bite-sized pieces

100g mangetout, each sliced into two on the diagonal

Juice of 1 lime

2 teaspoons fish sauce

Fresh coriander leaves

1 Heat the oil in a large saucepan and add the garlic. Fry over a medium heat for a couple of minutes, then pour the fish stock into the pan. Bring to the boil and add the chillies, lemongrass, coriander stalks and ginger. Reduce the stock to a simmer and allow all the ingredients to infuse for 15 minutes.

2 Carefully fish out the lemongrass and pour in the coconut milk. Bring to a simmer before adding the prawns, salmon and mangetout. Cook for just a couple of minutes until the fish is opaque and cooked through. Finally, stir in the lime juice and fish sauce. Serve with a delicate bundle of coriander and eat instantly.

BORLOTTI BEAN
TOMATO & SAGE SOUP

Most recipes for Italian-style tomato soup stand out with their basic technique of creating a *soffritto*, a simple melange of olive oil, celery, carrots and onion. This makes a wonderfully strong foundation to the soup upon which many ingredients can be added. Here is just one idea which happens to include my favourite bean. Eat with chunks of crusty bread, preferably while sitting on the sofa wrapped in a fleece.

PREP TIME 20 MINUTES   SERVES 6   COOK TIME 1 HOUR

100ml olive oil

3 sticks of celery, finely diced

2 carrots, peeled and finely diced

1 medium onion, finely diced

2 garlic cloves, peeled and finely chopped

5 or 6 sage leaves, roughly chopped, plus extra leaves
   to garnish

1 tablespoon tomato purée

1kg brilliant-quality tomatoes, roughly chopped
   into chunks

800ml vegetable stock

1 x 400g tin borlotti beans, drained and rinsed

1 Heat the olive oil in the base of a 3-litre casserole over a medium heat. Add the celery, carrots, onion, garlic and roughly chopped sage, reduce the heat to low and gently fry for approximately 15 minutes or until the vegetables have softened, stirring occasionally. Try not to get any colour on the vegetables as this is a gentle cooking process.

2 Add the tomato purée and stir in before adding the chopped tomatoes. Turn the heat to low and fry, covered, for a further 15 minutes, wiggling the pan every few minutes to prevent anything catching on the bottom. Pour over the stock and bring to the boil. Simmer for 30 minutes without a lid.

3 Using a stick blender, purée about half the soup so you are still left with some delicious chunks. Stir in the beans and cook for 2 minutes until your soup is heated through and the beans are warm. Garnish with deep-fried sage leaves (see tip).

 TIP – DEEP-FRIED SAGE LEAVES MAKE A QUICK AND DELICATE GARNISH FOR THIS SOUP. SIMPLY HEAT A COUPLE OF TABLESPOONS OF OIL IN A PAN UNTIL HOT, THEN DROP THE LEAVES IN FOR A FEW SECONDS. REMOVE THE LEAVES, DRAIN ON KITCHEN PAPER AND SPRINKLE WITH SALT.

CHILLY AVOCADO
CUCUMBER & YOGURT SOUP

Some might indulge in a spa visit to have cucumber slices laid on their eyes whilst whale music is played in the background, but my suggestion would be to save the money and rustle up the following. It's relaxingly simple, packed with all the right vitamins and, as the expression goes, 'cool as a cucumber'.

PREP TIME 15 MINUTES   **ENOUGH FOR 6 SMALL BOWLS**   COOK TIME 5 MINUTES

1 tablespoon butter

1 onion, roughly chopped

2 garlic cloves, peeled and squashed

1 litre cold vegetable stock

1 cucumber, peeled, chopped and the seeds scooped out

1 large very ripe avocado or 2 smaller ones, peeled, stoned and roughly chopped

3 tablespoons chopped mint

250ml thick Greek yogurt

A few drops of Tabasco (optional)

Sea salt and freshly ground black pepper

A handful of ice cubes and mint leaves, to serve

1 Melt the butter in a heavy-bottomed saucepan and add the chopped onion. Cook over a gentle heat for a few minutes until the onion has softened but not coloured. Add the garlic to the pot and cook for a further minute.

2 Remove from the heat and add the cold stock, cucumber chunks, avocado and chopped mint. Simply whiz using a stick blender or food processor – now you see how easy it is.

3 Stir through the Greek yogurt until you reach your desired creaminess. Season to taste and add the Tabasco if you fancy a bit of heat.

4 Serve in bowls over ice cubes and garnish with mint leaves. Now all you need is for the sun to come out.

APPLE & PARSNIP
SOUP

There is something effortlessly comforting about apples and parsnips; here they are combined in an elegant partnership perfect for an autumnal lunch. Do try the parsnip crisps, as they are the proverbial 'icing on the cake' and will provide an excellent and decorative use for the skin. Waste not, want not, as my father would say.

PREP TIME 25 MINUTES | **MAKES 4 BIG BOWLS OR 6 GIRLIE PORTIONS** | COOK TIME 1 HOUR 10 MINUTES

1 tablespoon salted butter

1 large onion, roughly chopped

1 teaspoon ground cumin

A trickle of runny honey

750g parsnips (about 5), peeled and cut into 2cm dice (keep the peelings for the crisps)

1 medium potato, peeled and cut into 2cm dice

2 healthy-sized green apples, peeled, cored and cut into 2cm dice

1.2 litres vegetable stock

Plain yogurt or parsnip crisps (see tip below), to serve

Sea salt and freshly ground black pepper

1 Melt the butter in a 3-litre saucepan over a gentle heat. Add the onion and cumin and sauté for a couple of minutes until the onion is translucent. Stir in the honey and allow it to bubble for a few moments.

2 Add the parsnips, potato and apple chunks and stir so all the pieces are coated in the cumin honey.

3 Pour over the hot vegetable stock and allow to simmer, covered, for an hour. Stir occasionally to make sure your soup is cooking evenly.

4 When everything is soft and the vegetables cut like butter, simply whiz using a stick blender. If you like the soup thinner, loosen with either milk or hot water. Add a good pinch of salt and a grating of black pepper. Return to the stove to heat through and then serve with a good dollop of yogurt or some parsnip crisps.

TIP – TO MAKE THE PARSNIP CRISPS, SIMPLY POUR APPROXIMATELY 3 TABLESPOONS VEGETABLE OIL INTO A DEEP FRYING PAN. HEAT OVER A HIGH FLAME AND ADD THE PARSNIP PEELINGS. SPRINKLE A GENEROUS AMOUNT OF SALT OVER THE PEELINGS AND ALLOW TO SIZZLE. DON'T BE TEMPTED TO MOVE THEM AROUND TOO MUCH – JUST EVERY MINUTE OR SO. THEY SHOULD TAKE 4–5 MINUTES TO CRISP UP. DRAIN ON KITCHEN PAPER AND THROW A GOOD BUNDLE ON TOP OF THE SOUP.

JUST VEGGIES

I was once told this old story that makes me smile. A young undergraduate was starting at Cambridge University. He and his fellow students arrived on day one to be met by a frosty-looking matron, who laid down a few ground rules to the boys: 'Now listen here', she bellowed, 'I will tolerate, every once in a while, you bringing girls back to your rooms. I will even turn a blind eye if you bring a man back to your room, but what I absolutely can't abide is vegetarians.'

Luckily I don't share this opinion; in fact, vegetarian food is to be relished. I hope you enjoy the following clutch of recipes, some of which take moments, while others require a wee bit of planning, but all, I promise, are delicious.

POLENTA BAKE
WITH TOMATO, FETA & MUSHROOMS

Years ago, ground polenta simply provided hunger-defying gruel to the poor, but today it's found cooked with the expensive additions of Parmesan and butter. The transformation has put it back on the map of Michelin-starred menus and into the repertoire of enthusiastic cooks. Here, instant polenta is used, so there are only minutes from packet to plate and the peasant price tag still holds strong. It's well worth stocking a packet in your store cupboard.

PREP TIME 10 MINUTES	SERVES 6	COOK TIME 20 MINUTES

150g instant polenta

50g unsalted butter, cut into chunks

750ml hot vegetable stock

60g Parmesan cheese, finely grated

100g mushrooms (any type really; my preference would be mini portabella), thinly sliced

150g cherry tomatoes, some halved, some not

100g feta cheese, crumbled

A handful of delicate rocket

Sea salt and freshly ground black pepper

1 Preheat your grill to high.

2 Put the polenta and chunks of butter in the bottom of a deep, 25cm-diameter, ovenproof frying pan over a medium heat. Gradually pour the hot stock onto the polenta, beating with gusto to prevent any large lumps forming. Keep beating until the mixture has thickened and is starting to bubble like erupting volcanoes, about 4–5 minutes. Season well with black pepper and salt.

3 Remove the pan from the heat and stir through the Parmesan. You could clean the sides of your frying pan at this stage to remove any obvious volcano larva (spitting polenta). Top the polenta with the mushroom slices, tomatoes and crumbled feta.

4 Put the pan under the hot grill for 10–12 minutes until the tomato skins have burst and the mushrooms have wilted with the heat. Allow to cool for a few minutes before dressing with rocket to serve.

 TIP – YOU WILL SEE PARMESAN CHEESE HAS BEEN USED TO ADD FLAVOUR BUT OF COURSE ANY FULL-FLAVOURED CHEESE WOULD BE DELICIOUS. USE A VEGETARIAN VARIETY IF YOU'RE ABLE TO TRACK IT DOWN.

PEARLED SPELT RISOTTO
WITH WATERCRESS & LEMON

There is a certain thrill to discovering fresh watercress swimming in docile English rivers, gesturing the beginning of spring. It is so green, peppery and robust that it can stand out by itself. Here, we have a simple spelt risotto in which the watercress is the star of the show. I'd eat it with a chunky wedge of garlic bread.

PREP TIME 10 MINUTES   SERVES 4   COOK TIME 30 MINUTES

25g butter

1 tablespoon olive oil

1 onion, finely chopped

2 garlic cloves, peeled and finely chopped

200g pearled spelt (alternatively, use risotto rice)

125ml dry white wine

1 litre hot vegetable stock

75g bunch of watercress, washed and roughly chopped

Grated zest and juice of 1 lemon

50g Parmesan, grated

Sea salt and freshly ground black pepper

A few rounds of goat's cheese, to serve

1 Heat half of the butter and all the oil in a large pan. Add the chopped onion and garlic and cook over a low heat, stirring occasionally, for 5 minutes or until softened. Add the pearled spelt (or risotto rice) and stir for 1 minute until the grains are coated in the buttery oil.

2 Pour in the wine and simmer over a high heat until nearly all has evaporated. A word of warning: there are times for drinking alcohol, but not within a risotto – take the time to allow the alcohol to evaporate.

3 Reduce the heat to gentle and begin to add the hot stock, a ladleful at a time, letting each ladleful be absorbed before adding the next. Keep adding the stock and stirring constantly until all of the liquid has been absorbed. This will take 18–20 minutes.

4 Remove the risotto from the heat and add the remaining butter, the chopped watercress, lemon zest and juice and the Parmesan. Stir until the watercress has just wilted, check for seasoning, and then serve with a round or two of goat's cheese resting on top.

BASIL, NUTMEG
& RICOTTA CANNELLONI

Fresh pasta used to be confined to specialist delicatessens, served only by olive-skinned Italians, but, as they often do, supermarkets have made this ingredient accessible to all of us. The recipe here forges strong Italian ingredients to create a dish that can only be described as '*molto bene*'.

PREP TIME 30 MINUTES   SERVES 6   COOK TIME 1 HOUR

500g fresh ricotta cheese, drained of any excess water

A good bunch of basil (30g)

½ nutmeg, grated, or 1 teaspoon ground nutmeg

50g Parmesan cheese, grated

225g fresh Italian vine tomatoes, roughly chopped

700ml passata (the more homemade the better)

250g fresh pasta sheets

4–5 spring onions, finely chopped

Sea salt and freshly ground black pepper

1 Preheat the oven to 180°C/gas mark 4.

2 In a large bowl, gently combine the ricotta, basil, nutmeg, half of the Parmesan and the roughly chopped tomatoes. Season well. Pour half of the passata in the base of a 2-litre ovenproof dish.

3 Cut the pasta sheets into individual rectangles (approximately 13 x 10cm) – don't worry too much if they aren't these exact measurements, as every pasta sheet varies in size. Lay these rectangles on your work top like a patchwork blanket and put 2 heaped tablespoons of the ricotta mixture along one edge of each rectangle. Roll up and place in your dish, join-side down to secure them. Keep going until you have used all the filling and pasta sheets. It doesn't matter if you have to pile them up a bit, but make sure the bottom layer is snug.

4 Cover with the remaining passata and sprinkle over the spring onions and the rest of the Parmesan. Give the dish a good grating of black pepper. Cover with greased foil and bake for 1 hour.

ORZO WITH MINT
& SUN-DRIED TOMATOES

Orzo is a tiny rice-shaped pasta traditionally used in Italian soups, but it's very versatile and cooks in minutes. I've used it here in a warm salad, and given it a bit more oomph by adding sun-dried tomatoes and mint. This dish will be on your table faster than it takes to call for a takeaway.

PREP TIME 5 MINUTES · · · · · · · · · · · SERVES 4 · · · · · · · · · · · COOK TIME 20 MINUTES

350g orzo
125g cream cheese
150g young leaf spinach

A bunch of mint (approx. 25g), chopped (reserve a few whole leaves for garnish)
100g sun-dried tomatoes, roughly chopped
Sea salt and freshly ground black pepper

1 Heat a large pan of boiling water and drop the orzo into the water. Stir vigorously at once, to prevent the little grains sticking, and then stir occasionally during cooking. Simmer for 8 minutes. Scoop out 100ml of the cooking water and set aside.

2 Drain the orzo and return to the pot with the reserved cooking water. Keep the pot over a very gentle heat while you add the cream cheese and spinach leaves. Stir until the spinach has wilted and the cheese has coated the grains. Add the chopped mint and sun-dried tomatoes. Season with salt and freshly ground black pepper.

3 Serve with a fresh mint leaf or two over the top.

FRESHLY GRATED
ASIAN SALAD

Nothing is as virtuous as an Asian salad: fresh, crunchy vegetables tossed lightly with a tangy dressing and embellished with roasted peanuts. A friend, Belle, taught me how to fashion Asian cuisine from weathered English ingredients so I have her to thank for this refreshing dish.

PREP TIME 20 MINUTES   SERVES 4

400g cucumber

1 red pepper, cut into the thinnest strips possible

150g beansprouts

1 large carrot, peeled and grated

1 teaspoon fish sauce

1 tablespoon rice vinegar

2 tablespoons vegetable oil

1 tablespoon seriously finely chopped lemongrass

3 tablespoons lime juice

1 tablespoon palm sugar or dark brown sugar

1 tablespoon finely chopped mint, plus extra leaves
   to garnish

40g roasted peanuts, chopped

1 First, prepare the cucumber. Cut it in half lengthways, then scoop out the seeds (I find a teaspoon does the best job of this) and discard. Cut each hollowed length into three equal chunks and then each chunk into thin strips. Toss with the red pepper strips, beansprouts and grated carrot and set aside.

2 To make the dressing, put the fish sauce, rice vinegar, vegetable oil, lemongrass, lime juice, sugar and chopped mint in a small bowl and stir to combine, or shake together in a closed jam jar.

3 Put all the ingredients except the peanuts in a large bowl and toss together. Sprinkle over the dressing and dust with the peanuts. Job done.

COUNTRYSIDE POT

PREP TIME 10 MINUTES • COOK TIME 25 MINUTES

Salads have moved on a long way since the days of a limp Caesar or Niçoise. Forgive me – these recipes are wonderful for the correct moment, but with the wealth of seasonal ingredients available it's fitting that salads can meander down many different paths. Here, we have a hearty salad, a rugby player's equivalent of the traditional green side, which requires only a chunk of dripping Brie and a generous dollop of chutney.

SERVES 4–6

1kg new potatoes, the bigger ones cut in half

200g green beans, topped

2 x 400g tins borlotti beans, drained and rinsed

1 red onion, sliced into thin slivers

A good handful of flat-leaf parsley, roughly chopped

Grated zest of 1 lemon

FOR THE DRESSING

2 tablespoons Dijon mustard

120ml olive oil

60ml cider vinegar

2 teaspoons caster sugar

1 Put the potatoes in a saucepan of cold water and bring to a simmer. Cook for approximately 20 minutes or until they are tender. Pop the green beans into the pan for the last 3–4 minutes so they are just tender but still with a little crunch.

2 Make your dressing by combining all the ingredients and stirring, or shaking, until perfectly emulsified.

3 Drain the beans and potatoes. Return to the pan and stir through the borlotti beans, red onion and dressing. Sprinkle over the parsley and lemon zest and serve.

PANZANELLA

PREP TIME 45 MINUTES

Panzanella is the salad world's response to bread recycling. Don't discard aged loaves as if they are models teetering on the age of thirty; in fact, the slightly drier the bread, the better the salad. Watch as the ciabatta soaks up freshly escaped tomato juice and a tart red wine vinegar dressing to become a scrumptious base to this summer recipe.

SERVES 4

300g 1- or 2-day-old bread (ciabatta is best)

3 ripe beef tomatoes

1 small red onion, finely chopped

2 garlic cloves, peeled and crushed

1 medium cucumber, chopped in four lengthways, then sliced

A handful of caperberries

60ml extra-virgin olive oil

60ml red wine vinegar

1 ball of tender buffalo mozzarella, torn into bite-sized chunks

A handful of basil and mint leaves

Sea salt and freshly ground black pepper

1 Tear or cube the bread into 2–3cm chunks and put into a large bowl. Roughly chop the tomatoes, keeping all the lovely juices that try to run away, and add to the bowl with the onion, garlic, cucumber and caperberries. Toss lightly to combine and evenly distribute all the ingredients.

2 Mix together the olive oil and vinegar and pour over the bread and tomato mixture. Leave to sit for 20 minutes in the fridge so all the flavours have a chance to socialise.

3 Just before serving, toss through the mozzarella, basil and mint leaves. Season and serve, preferably when you are holidaying in Italy, or want to be!

BULGUR WHEAT
BEETROOT & AVOCADO SALAD

Beetroot is having a renaissance and why shouldn't it? The intense colour, earthy flavour and remarkable health properties have put it firmly on the superfoods map. If eating it raw, just scrub clean, grate as you would a carrot and forget any distant memories of jarred, pickled beetroot which may cloud your opinion. Catch the beetroot before it wrinkles and the skin turns into that of an old man; you've got about a week before it starts looking sad.

PREP TIME 20 MINUTES · SERVES 4–6 · COOK TIME 15 MINUTES

150g bulgur wheat

500g raw beetroot (approx. 4), peeled or aggressively scrubbed

2 ripe avocados, peeled, stoned and sliced

1 red onion, finely sliced

4 tablespoons chopped dill

4 tablespoons extra virgin olive oil

3 tablespoons white wine vinegar

½ teaspoon caster sugar

½ teaspoon Tabasco

1 teaspoon wholegrain mustard

1 Place the bulgur wheat in a small pan with 600ml cold water. Bring to the boil and simmer for 12–15 minutes. Drain and fork through the grains to make sure you haven't got any nasty clumps.

2 Cut the beetroot as you wish. You could, for example, grate them, use the matchstick chopper on a food processor or use your knife skills to slice them into matchsticks by hand. One piece of advice is to use rubber gloves to prevent unwanted stains on your hands.

3 Lightly toss together the bulgur wheat, beetroot, avocados, red onion and dill. In a small jug, combine the olive oil, vinegar, caster sugar, Tabasco and mustard. Drizzle the dressing over the salad, which is now ready to serve (but not to anybody wearing white!).

RICOTTA & WHITE BEAN MEDLEY

PREP TIME 15 MINUTES

My sister, Caroline, gets married this year and we've had many crucial conversations about the implications of a white or off-white wedding dress. This dish made me think of her. Startling white ricotta clouds are tossed with golden-white cannellini beans, each competing to catch the eye. Other summer ingredients are the sunshine backdrop to a jolly simple, yet scrumptious dish.

SERVES 4

1 x 400g tin cannellini beans, drained and rinsed

3–4 spring onions, sliced on the diagonal

150g cherry tomatoes, halved

1 large red chilli, deseeded and finely sliced

75g black olives, pitted

3 tablespoons olive oil

2 tablespoons balsamic vinegar

100g pea shoots

100g fresh ricotta cheese

Sea salt and freshly ground black pepper

1 Lightly toss the cannellini beans, spring onions, cherry tomtatoes, chilli and olives in a big bowl. Drizzle over the olive oil and balsamic vinegar and toss to coat.

2 Gently add the pea shoots, handling them like thin glass to try to avoid bruising the leaves.

3 Arrange in a lovely dish and dollop the ricotta over the salad. Punctuate with salt and pepper and serve.

GOAT'S CHEESE & SPRING ONION FETTUCCINE

PREP TIME 10 MINUTES • COOK TIME 15 MINUTES

One Sunday morning four of us embarked on a significant 10-mile run, along the tarmacked roads from Waterloo to London Fields. The reward was a lengthy swim in the outdoor lido and this lunch on our return home.

SERVES 4

500g fettuccine

50g very soft butter

50g Parmesan cheese, finely grated

75g creamy, rindless goat's cheese

A large bunch of spring onions, finely chopped on the diagonal

150g hazelnuts, toasted until a little charred

Sea salt and freshly ground black pepper

1 First point. Read through the recipe. This one is quick, but it relies on you being organised! Don't cook the pasta until you have all the sauce ingredients ready to go.

2 Bring a large saucepan of water to the boil. When the water starts to simmer, drop the pasta in and cook for a few minutes until al dente. Be careful not to overcook the pasta: this dish needs a little bite to it. While the pasta is cooking, scoop out 200ml of the cooking liquid and keep aside.

3 Drain the pasta thoroughly, then return the empty pan to a low heat. Working quickly, add the reserved water, softened butter, Parmesan, goat's cheese and spring onions (reserving a few for the garnish). Cook over a medium heat for a minute or so, stirring constantly, until the cheese and butter coat the pasta. Season well with sea salt and freshly ground black pepper. Remove from the heat and stir in the hazelnuts. Serve straight away, garnished with the reserved spring onions.

PERFECTLY PUFFED
CHEESE & BREAD POT

My Canadian friend, Andrea, taught me this recipe. Her 'mom' used to make it on Christmas Day morning, to be eaten bleary-eyed amid the excitement, bursting stockings and chilled champagne. Everything should be prepared the night before, so the humble ingredients have time to mingle and be transformed from a relatively ordinary cluster into an exceptionally yummy dish. The magic of Christmas perhaps?

PREP TIME 20 MINUTES
(PLUS OVERNIGHT SOAKING)

SERVES 6

COOK TIME 50 MINUTES

2 tablespoons very soft butter, plus extra for greasing

4–6 slices of white bread (2–3cm thick), crusts removed (approx. 150g crustless weight)

100g mature Cheddar cheese, coarsely grated

2 medium free-range eggs

300ml semi-skimmed milk

Sea salt and freshly ground black pepper

1 Use some of the soft butter to grease a 1-litre, ovenproof soufflé dish; I always find my fingers the most useful implement to do this with.

2 Butter the slices of bread, then cube into postage stamp-sized pieces (approx. 3 x 3cm). There should be enough to fill the soufflé dish three-quarters full. Put into the dish, add the grated cheese and, using your hands, combine so the cheese is evenly distributed.

3 Crack the eggs into a small bowl and beat lightly using a hand whisk. Add the milk and whisk for 2–3 minutes. Season well. Slowly pour over the bread-and-cheese mixture. Cover and pop in the fridge overnight.

4 All the hard work has been done. The next day, all that's needed is to preheat the oven to 200°C/gas mark 6 and bake the soufflé for 40 minutes or until golden and puffed like a peacock.

SWEET POTATO
& COCONUT DHAL

Whoever said lentils were bland? With the addition of just a few delicate spices this recipe makes for a beautifully aromatic and chunky dhal: a delicious accompaniment for a curry or a simple lunch to take to the office. Be sure to transform yours with a generous spoonful of Greek yogurt and some torn coriander; after all, even a simple dhal deserves to be dressed for the table.

PREP TIME 15 MINUTES
(PLUS OVERNIGHT SOAKING)　　　SERVES 6 (SIDE) OR 4 (MAIN)　　　COOK TIME 1 HOUR

200g yellow split peas

1 tablespoon olive oil

1 onion, finely chopped

½ teaspoon chilli flakes

1 teaspoon garam masala

1 teaspoon ground turmeric

1 teaspoon ground cumin

3cm piece of fresh ginger, peeled and chopped

400ml coconut milk

300g sweet potatoes, peeled and chopped into
   small cubes

1 x 400g tin chopped tomatoes

150ml vegetable stock

3 tablespoons chopped fresh coriander leaves

2 tablespoons whole almonds

Sea salt and freshly ground black pepper

1 Cover the split peas with cold water and soak overnight. The following morning, drain, rinse and set aside.

2 Heat the olive oil in a deep casserole. Add the onion and cook over a medium heat for a couple of minutes until it begins to caramelise. Add the chilli flakes, garam masala, turmeric, cumin and chopped ginger to the pot and cook for another minute to soften the ginger.

3 Add the coconut milk, split peas, diced sweet potatoes, chopped tomatoes and vegetable stock. Season well, cover and simmer for 1 hour until the dhal is deliciously thick and the lentils are falling apart. Top up with more hot stock if you think the dahl is becoming dry. Serve with the chopped coriander and whole almonds.

SLOW-BAKED POTATO DAUPHINOISE

PREP TIME 15 MINUTES • COOK TIME 3 HOURS

The name 'dauphinoise' originates from the Dauphine area of France. It is a mere coincidence that this regal dish is similar to 'dauphin', the name bestowed upon the heir to the French throne. With all this history, it seems fitting that I would describe it as my 'King of Sides'. Cream, potato and garlic, all baked very slowly, then ripening until the top is crowned with gold. Long live the monarchy!

SERVES 8

Butter, for greasing

300ml double cream

300ml crème fraîche (not low-fat as this will split during cooking)

100ml semi-skimmed milk

3 large garlic cloves, peeled and crushed

1 onion, thinly sliced into rings

1kg floury potatoes, peeled and sliced into 3–4 mm slices (or as near as you can get!)

Sea salt and freshly ground black pepper

1 Preheat the oven to 150°C/gas mark 2. Lightly butter a 2-litre ovenproof dish.

2 In a small jug, combine the cream, crème fraîche, milk and garlic and allow to infuse for a few minutes.

3 Layer up the sliced potato and onion rings to cover the bottom of your dish. Season well, then continue to add layers until all the potato and onion slices have been used. Slowly pour over the creamy mixture, allowing each addition to find the crevices and disappear before adding more. Season again.

4 Bake in the oven for 3 hours.

A SIDE OF SPICED SWEET POTATO & PARSNIPS

PREP TIME 30 MINUTES • COOK TIME 45 MINUTES

If this recipe were to be featured in a lonely-hearts column, the entry might looks something like this: 'A plain vegetable seeks a vibrant fish to add interest to his relationship; despite dressing simply and despite much of life spent underground, he is willing to be served hot.' Don't let the appearances of these two root vegetables put you off. A sprinkling of chilli, garlic and rosemary and a viciously hot oven will transform them and they will be perfect with any roasted joint you cook.

PLENTY FOR 6

1 teaspoon cayenne pepper

700g sweet potatoes, scrubbed

700g parsnips, scrubbed and sliced into quarters lengthways

½ teaspoon chilli flakes

6 garlic cloves, bashed but not peeled

3 sprigs of rosemary

2 tablespoons olive oil

Sea salt and freshly ground black pepper

1 Preheat the oven to 200°C/gas mark 6.

2 Place all the ingredients in a roasting tray and mix. Don't be afraid to get your hands involved as you'll achieve the best coating that way. Season well.

3 Roast for 45 minutes, turning half way through.

CREAMY ROASTED LEEK
& CAULIFLOWER

Cauliflower, with its mild and homely sort of flavour, is not one to steal the spotlight on a menu, but can be relied upon if it's given a moment's thought. I ate my fair share of cauliflower cheese throughout my childhood but feel that it deserves a makeover, and I'd argue this recipe is easier. It may take longer in the oven, but with no white sauce to contend with it is quick, simple and exquisitely tasty.

PREP TIME 10 MINUTES | **SERVES 6 (SIDE) OR 4 (MAIN)** | COOK TIME 1 HOUR

1 x 800g cauliflower, divided into small florets about the size of a ping-pong ball

2 medium leeks, cut in half lengthways and then into 1–2cm crescents

½ teaspoon cumin seeds (optional)

2–3 tablespoons oil

100ml crème fraîche

150ml double cream

2 teaspoons Dijon mustard

125g strong, punchy Cheddar cheese

Sea salt and freshly ground black pepper

1 Preheat the oven to 200°C/gas mark 6. The key to this recipe is that the oven is hot, so if you're not completely confident your oven gets to that temperature, crank it up a few degrees and keep a watchful eye on the dish!

2 Put the cauliflower, leeks and cumin seeds into a large metal roasting tin. Coat with oil and give the whole lot a good jumble. Cover tightly with foil and roast in the hot oven for 40 minutes.

3 Take out of the oven and remove the foil; the leeks will have wilted and the cauliflower will be soft and steamy. Give everything a good stir.

4 Reduce the oven temperature to 180°C/gas mark 4. Spoon over the crème fraîche, double cream and mustard and a healthy grinding of salt and pepper. Using a big spoon, mix everything together so it looks like a snowy mountain range. Sprinkle over the cheese then cook for a further 20 minutes until the top is perfectly golden.

HOLLOWED SQUASH
WITH LENTILS, COURGETTE & BLUE CHEESE

While I was living in Zimbabwe, butternut squash became as familiar a staple as bread and butter. We'd roast it, blitz it, make chocolate brownies from it… but there was always one winner and that was to stuff it. Like the African lifestyle, this recipe is happy to sit and chill for a little while once it escapes from the oven, making it perfect for entertaining. The recipe has a two-step process, so is perfect for making a day or two in advance.

PREP TIME 30 MINUTES   SERVES 4   COOK TIME 30 MINUTES

1 large butternut squash
1 small courgette
75g crème fraîche
150g Stilton, crumbled

1 x 400g tin green lentils, drained
1 tablespoon chopped flat-leaf parsley
Sea salt and freshly ground black pepper

1 Preheat the oven to 180°C/gas mark 4.

2 Cut the butternut squash in half lengthways and scoop out the seeds and discard. Place, flesh-side down, on an oiled baking sheet and bake for 30 minutes.

3 Meanwhile, prepare the filling. Slice the courgette in half lengthways and then chop into 0.5cm crescents. Place in a bowl with the crème fraîche, 100g of the crumbled Stilton, the lentils and parsley. Season, season, season. Cover and place in the fridge until needed.

4 Remove the squash from the oven – the flesh should be softening slightly but still have a bit of bite to it. Leave for a few minutes until cool enough to the touch, then use a spoon to gently remove the flesh from the centre of

the squash. Don't veer too near the sides – allow 1–2cm around the edge – as you don't want the squash to collapse. Dice the flesh and add to the chilled mixture. (Stop here if preparing the dish in advance.)

5 Spoon the courgette-and-squash loveliness into the hollowed-out squash halves. Keep on piling it in, pushing it down and piling it in: it will fit, I'm sure of it. Finish by sprinkling the remaining Stilton over the top and return to the oven to cook for a further 30 minutes.

6 I suggest leaving the squash halves to sit for 10 minutes or so when they come out of the oven, as this allows the delicious liquid to be soaked up by the vegetables.

AUBERGINE RACKS
WITH HALLOUMI, LEMON & THYME

In my humble opinion, aubergines get a raw deal – they are known for nothing more than Greek mousaka and Turkish baba ganoush, but I believe the silky purple orbs should be treated with respect. Here is a creative way of cooking aubergines that takes no time to prepare and lets the oven (or fire) do its work. Serve for lunch with a simple pile of dressed rocket.

PREP TIME 10 MINUTES
PLUS 1 HOUR MARINATING

SERVES 3–4 AS A SIDE

COOK TIME 1 HOUR

2 large aubergines

Juice of 1 large lemon

2 tablespoons extra virgin olive oil

½ red onion, sliced into thin rings

125g halloumi cheese, sliced into 0.5–1cm slices

1 small, fresh red chilli, deseeded and finely chopped

8 sprigs of thyme

Freshly ground black pepper

1 Place each aubergine in turn on a chopping board and allow it to fall on its side. Gently slice vertically at 1.5cm intervals, cutting deep into the flesh but taking care not to slice all the way through to the bottom.

2 Sprinkle the lemon juice and olive oil all over the aubergine, making sure they drizzle into the cracks. Leave for an hour or so to ensure the flesh soaks up all those beautiful flavours.

3 Preheat the oven to 200°C/gas mark 6.

4 When you are ready, stuff the onion rings and halloumi into alternate slits in the aubergines as if you're putting toast in a toast rack. Don't worry if they poke above the aubergine – it will sort itself out in the oven. Scatter over the red chilli, squeeze the thyme stalks amongst the racks and give them a good grinding of black pepper.

5 Place the aubergines on oiled foil and enclose in a parcel shape. Bake in the oven for 45 minutes. Open the parcel and roast for a further 15 minutes.

 TIP – THE MARINATING TIME IN THIS RECIPE IS IMPORTANT – IT BEGINS TO BREAK DOWN THE AUBERGINE FLESH. DON'T BE TEMPTED TO DO LESS THAN AN HOUR, BUT OF COURSE YOU COULD LEAVE THEM OVERNIGHT IF IT HELPED EASE PREPARATIONS ON THE DAY.

OEUFS EN COCOTTE WITH SORREL & GARLIC

PREP TIME 5 MINUTES • COOK TIME 20 MINUTES

'Baked eggs' might be a more familiar title for this recipe but I think that the French translation reads more romantically, as it so often does. Just five ingredients sit together flawlessly and require but a moment's preparation – a lemony edge of sorrel and a kick of garlic cut through the delicate egg and cream, making for a yummy, very miniature one-pot.

SERVES 4

Butter, for greasing
A handful of fresh sorrel, roughly chopped (or replace with wilted spinach and the zest of 1 lemon)
4 tablespoons double cream
1 garlic clove, peeled and very well crushed
4 large free-range eggs
A few sprigs of dill or chervil
Sea salt and freshly ground black pepper

1 Preheat the oven to 180°C/gas mark 4. Lightly butter the inside of 4 x 250ml ramekins.

2 In a small jug, lightly beat together the sorrel, cream and garlic and season with sea salt flakes and plenty of black pepper. Pour your mixture into the ramekins and crack an egg on top of each. Garnish with dill or chervil.

3 Place the ramekins in a roasting tin, then pour enough boiling water into the tin to reach half way up the ramekins – this creates a lovely, steamy environment for the eggs so there is no chance of them drying out. Carefully transfer to the oven and cook for 15–20 minutes.

4 Serve with a good grinding of black pepper.

QUICHE IN A SUITCASE

PREP TIME 15 MINUTES • COOK TIME 1 HOUR

One of my oldest friends, Jenny, lives near Borough Market – just close enough to smell the charred chorizo and indulge in a roast pork roll more often than necessary. During one morning spent there I talked to a baker about the possibility of making a quiche within a hollowed loaf, rather than pastry. Could it be done? Yes it can.

SERVES 8

1 large boule of bread, approx. 25cm round and 800g in weight
6 medium free-range eggs
300ml double cream
125g mature Cheddar cheese, grated
250g cherry tomatoes, halved horizontally
25g fresh basil, roughly chopped
Sea salt and freshly ground black pepper

1 Preheat the oven to 160°C/gas mark 3. Cut about a third off the top of the loaf of bread to give a depth of 6–8cm for the filling. Hollow out the inside by removing 90 per cent of the crumb, but be careful not to make the shell too thin or it might not stand up to the filling; about 1cm thick is perfect. (Now what could you do with the inside? Bread sauce, croûtons, a treacle tart – or see page 33 for a quick panzanella.)

2 Crack the eggs into a medium-sized bowl and lightly beat with a fork. Then simply pour in the double cream and add two-thirds each of the Cheddar, tomatoes and basil. Season heavily.

3 Pour into your prepared suitcase. There should be about a 2.5cm clearance from the top of the mixture to the lip of the bread. Dress the top of the mixture with the remaining cheese, tomatoes and basil. Give a good grinding of black pepper and bake for 1 hour or until the filling is firm to the touch. Turn off the oven and allow the quiche to cool inside. To serve, simply slice into wedges.

FISH FOOD

Not long ago, I spent a sunny day surfing off the Cornish coast. We lay lethargically sunbathing on boards, limbs dangling, hopeful that the unobliging sea would cough up some waves or at least entertainment§. Then I started to get nervous. My mother is right; why does one don fancy dress, willingly lie in deep water disguised as seals and wait to be attacked? Perhaps it's natural, but I do find all of those fishes, molluscs, unknown and undiscovered things that reside in water quite intimidating.

The same could be said of a fish counter. We go back, time after time, like bees to a honey pot, choosing the same old fish, never venturing near an unfamiliar shape or odd-looking flat fish. A little bit of know-how and these fish seem far more approachable, so I hope you might take a few minutes to choose a recipe that takes you a small step away from your comfort zone. You never know, you may just surprise yourself.

STEAMED SALMON

ON A BED OF BEANS, CHILLI & COURGETTE

When a chef declares that the main has been cooked *en papillotte*, you might think that he or she is worthy of admiration. But for those in the know, this culinary technique is as simple as wrapping a present. It merely means creating a parcel that speedily steams the food – generally fish, fruit or vegetables – and seals in the flavours. All that the guests have to do is unwrap their gift.

PREP TIME 10 MINUTES   SERVES 2   COOK TIME 25 MINUTES

1 x 400g tin kidney beans, drained and rinsed

1 small courgette, grated

3 garlic cloves, peeled and finely chopped

2 fresh red chillies, deseeded and finely chopped
   (reserve a little to garnish)

½ teaspoon black onion seeds, plus extra for sprinkling

Grated zest and juice of 1 lemon

1 tablespoon chervil leaves (use dill if you can't find
   any chervil), plus extra for garnish

2 teaspoons Dijon mustard

2 salmon fillets, skinned

2 teaspoons butter

2 tablespoons dry white wine

Sea salt and freshly ground black pepper

1 Preheat the oven to 190°C/gas mark 5.

2 In a bowl combine the kidney beans, courgette, garlic, chilli, black onion seeds, lemon zest and juice, chervil (or dill) and mustard, giving everything a good jumble. Season this mixture well.

3 Lay two lengths of baking parchment or foil, about 35cm long, on your work surface. Split the vegetable mixture in half and spoon on top of each piece of foil. Nestle a salmon fillet in the middle, season, and then top with the butter, a sprinkling of onion seeds and a scattering of chervil.

4 Seal the sides of the parcel, leaving a small gap to pour 1 tablespoon of wine into each, then seal completely. Make sure that there aren't any holes as it's the contained steam that will cook the contents – if there is an accidental tear, wrap with another piece of baking parchment/foil.

5 Pop in the oven for 25 minutes. Tear open the parcel and serve with the rest of the bottle of wine. Idyllic.

BAKED WHOLE SEA BASS
WITH AUBERGINE & TAMARIND

Some recipes can't be bracketed into particular continents. As Anna Hansen – chef at the Modern Pantry in London – believes, ingredients aren't specific to certain countries, 'they are simply a worldwide storecupboard'. Here, we have a Thai-Indian recipe that is stuffed with big, global flavours. It's a no-fuss way of cooking fish that makes for a wonderfully rustic meal.

PREP TIME 20 MINUTES   SERVES 4–6   COOK TIME 35 MINUTES

3 tablespoons olive oil

3 small onions, thinly sliced

1 large aubergine, cut into 3cm cubes

3 garlic cloves, peeled and thinly sliced

½ tablespoon curry powder

3cm chunk of fresh ginger, peeled and grated

½ tablespoon tamarind, mixed with 2 tablespoons
   boiling water

2 hot red chillies (or as many or as few as you wish),
   cut into chunky diagonals

6 medium tomatoes, cut into quarters

300ml coconut milk

4 small sea bass, scaled and gutted, the heads removed

Fresh coriander, chopped

Sea salt and freshly ground black pepper

1 Preheat the oven to 200°C/gas mark 6. Put 2 tablespoons of the olive oil in a large ovenproof pot over a medium heat and fry the onions and aubergine. Allow to sizzle for about 8 minutes, until the aubergine begins to break down and look a little charred.

2 Add the garlic, curry powder and ginger and cook for a further minute. The pot should smell delicious. Now, simply stir through the tamarind, chillies, tomato quarters and coconut milk and remove from the heat.

3 Slash the fish three times on the diagonal on both sides and season well, not forgetting the cavity.

4 Snuggle the fish on top of your curry bed. (You could transfer to a roasting tin here if your initial pot isn't quite long enough.) Season again. Drizzle with the remaining oil and roast, uncovered, in the oven for 20–25 minutes. The flesh should be firm and crispy and the vegetables saucy and broken down.

5 Using a fish slice, remove the fish and, holding a sharp knife flat against the back bone, fillet each one.

6 Serve a pile of juicy vegetables with a fillet of sea bass alongside. Scatter with coriander to finish off the plate beautifully.

 TIP – IF YOU DON'T FEEL CONFIDENT FILLETING FISH ONCE IT'S COOKED, SIMPLY BUY SEA BASS FILLETS AND COOK THE VEGETABLES ALONE IN THE OVEN FOR 15 MINUTES, BEFORE ADDING THE FILLETS FOR A FURTHER 10 MINUTES.

WHITING, BUTTER BEAN
& RED PEPPER STEW

We are rapidly running out of our favourite fish. They have quite simply been eaten out of house and sea and as loyal fish eaters, it is time we gave the cods, tunas and salmons a chance to regroup and rebreed. Whiting can be just as plump as its cousinly cod and has a wonderfully delicate flavour, which will balance with the sweet red peppers.

PREP TIME 20 MINUTES   SERVES 4–6   COOK TIME 35 MINUTES

2 tablespoons olive oil

300g shallots, finely sliced

2 red peppers, sliced into 1–2cm lengths

3 garlic cloves, peeled and thinly sliced

1 teaspoon Spanish smoked paprika

200ml dry white wine

2 x 400g tins butter beans, rinsed and drained

Grated zest and juice of 1 lemon

3 tablespoons crème fraîche

75g black olives, pitted

500g whiting fillet, cut into chunks

2 tablespoons roughly chopped coriander

1 Heat the olive oil over a low heat in a 2-litre pot. Add the shallots, red peppers, garlic and paprika and fry gently, covered, until the vegetables soften. This needs to be a gentle process – try not to get any colour on the shallots – and can take a little while (about 15 minutes).

2 Pour in the wine, turn up the heat and bring to the boil to allow the alcohol to burn off and the liquid to reduce by half. Add the butter beans and lemon zest and juice to the pot. Cook through for a couple of minutes before returning to a gentle heat. Stir through the crème fraîche and olives and warm through.

3 Gently place the whiting fillets on top of the stew and cover with a lid. Steam over a low heat for 10–12 minutes until the fish is translucent and opaque all the way through. Remove the lid, turn off the heat and sprinkle over the coriander. Serve before the fish has any chance to overcook.

CARAMELISED FISH POT

This pot is inspired by fond memories of being engulfed by the sweet caramel aroma that lingers like fog in cities throughout Vietnam. On any visit, you'll notice caramel sauce is widely used in the country's cooking for braising to provide both an intense flavour and a deliciously glazed appearance to the finished food. Catfish is the traditional fish of choice for a fish pot, as the flesh is very meaty, but halibut is a good alternative and almost certainly easier to find.

PREP TIME 15 MINUTES   **SERVES 4**   COOK TIME 20 MINUTES

4 meaty white fish steaks (approx. 600g total weight),
   e.g. halibut, catfish or whiting

2 tablespoons fish sauce

3 tablespoons peanut or sesame oil

60g caster sugar

100g shallots, finely chopped

2 garlic cloves, peeled and sliced

5cm piece of fresh ginger, peeled and finely chopped

125ml coconut juice

1 fiery fresh red chilli, deseeded and finely chopped

3–4 spring onions, chopped

Sea salt and freshly ground black pepper

TO SERVE

Steamed rice

A good handful of Vietnamese mint

Lime wedges

1 Marinate the fish in a bowl with the fish sauce and just 1 tablespoon of the peanut or sesame oil and set aside while you start making the caramel sauce.

2 Heat the remaining oil in a heavy-based iron pot – or, if you are lucky enough to own a clay pot, this is the moment to get it out! Add the sugar and stir to combine. Keep the heat high and leave the mixture to caramelise. This can take some minutes, so be patient, stirring only every 30 seconds or so.

3 Once you have a lovely caramel emerging, throw in the shallots, garlic and ginger. Stir so they are completely coated before pouring in the coconut juice. Be careful: your pot will spit like an angry dragon. Some lumps of sugar may appear because the juice is cold, but continue to heat, stirring, until they disappear.

4 Add the marinated fish and chopped chillli and reduce the heat to medium/low. Cover with a lid and allow the fish to steam for 10–12 minutes.

5 Remove from the heat, adjust the seasoning, adding a little more fish sauce if you fancy, and stir through the spring onions. Serve in small bowls with the steamed rice, fresh mint and a lime wedge or two.

 TIP – THIS POT IS PREDOMINANTLY FISH AND IN ORDER TO BULK IT OUT A LITTLE I SUGGEST SERVING IT WITH SOME STEAMED RICE – A CARBOHYDRATE ACCOMPANIMENT WILL MAKE YOUR FISH STRETCH FAR FURTHER.

STUFFED MACKEREL
CURLS WITH CRUNCHY POTATOES

I think this recipe is incredible, with mackerel fillets transformed from quite a frugal understudy of an ingredient to the sophisticated star of the show. The end result is wonderfully healthy in an Italian sort of way, with plenty of olive oil, garlic, lemon and seasoning. Many a time we've enjoyed the leftovers a day afterwards, cold and bleached with purple, straight from a tupperware dish in the fridge.

PREP TIME 20 MINUTES   SERVES 6   COOK TIME 45 MINUTES

3 tablespoons extra virgin olive oil, plus extra for greasing

1.2kg waxy potatoes, scrubbed clean and cut into large chunks

1 head of garlic divided into cloves, the outer paper on each clove kept intact

250g cooked beetroot, grated (and any excess liquid squeezed away)

100g fresh, fluffy, white breadcrumbs

20g bunch of dill, roughly chopped

Grated zest and juice of 1 large lemon

6 mackerel fillets, skin on but pin-boned

Sea salt and freshly ground black pepper

100g plain thick yogurt, to serve

You will also need 6 wooden cocktail sticks

1 Preheat the oven to 200ºC/gas mark 6.

2 Rub a large roasting tin with a little oil to prevent any sticking. Throw in the potatoes and whole garlic cloves, drizzle with 2 tablespoons of the oil and season. Give the whole pan a good shake. Roast in the hot oven for 30 minutes, turning half way through to make sure the bottoms aren't catching.

3 Meanwhile, make the stuffing: combine the grated beetroot, breadcrumbs, half the chopped dill and the lemon zest in a small bowl and season well. Mix until the consistency is pliable and holds its shape – you could squeeze a little lemon juice in if it needs to be slightly more moist.

4 Lie the mackerel fillets on a board and top each one with a good spoonful of stuffing. Fold the fillet in half lengthways to encase the stuffing and secure with a cocktail stick. Don't worry if you have any left over stuffing – it can just be spooned over the potatoes.

5 Remove the potatoes from the oven and rest the six stuffed fillets on top. Spoon any leftover stuffing around the fillets and drizzle with the remaining olive oil. Roast for 12–15 minutes, or until the fish feels firm to the touch. Serve with a good spoonful of thick yogurt and the remaining dill.

BAKED SMOKED HADDOCK

WITH GNOCCHI & GREENS

Smoked haddock has a gutsy character, pushing it to prominence in any dish it chooses to star in. Here, pillows of gnocchi and delicate green vegetables act as supporting roles in a dish that might just become your 'new fish pie.'

PREP TIME 10 MINUTES   SERVES 3–4   COOK TIME 35 MINUTES

500g fresh gnocchi

200g baby courgettes, sliced at an angle into 0.5cm rounds, or 2 small courgettes, halved down the middle and chopped into crescents

250g asparagus, cut into 2cm lengths

200ml full-fat crème fraîche

1 tablespoon finely chopped dill

350g smoked haddock, skinned and cut into 2.5cm pieces

4 tablespoons Parmesan cheese, grated

Sea salt and freshly ground black pepper

1 One piece of advice, get everything ready beforehand because once you get going, this can be quite a quick recipe! Make sure you have a large, shallow pot that can go both on the hob and in the oven.

2 Preheat the oven to 200°C/gas mark 6.

3 Fill your pot with water and place on a high heat. Bring to the boil and add the gnocchi, courgettes and asparagus. Cook for 3 minutes, no more, no less, and drain.

4 Return the cooked gnocchi and vegetables to the pot and stir in the crème fraîche and dill. Next, a little more gently, add the pieces of smoked haddock. Combine until all the ingredients are evenly distributed and then give the dish a good season with black pepper and a little salt.

5 Scatter with the Parmesan and cook, covered, in the oven for 15–20 minutes, until the vegetables have softened but still retain a little bite. That's it… now you can put your feet up while your pot is happily cooking.

 TIP – A WORD OF WARNING: DON'T USE HALF FAT CRÈME FRAÎCHE AS SADLY IT WILL SPLIT DURING COOKING.

RICE NOODLE
PRAWN & FRESH HERB SALAD

This recipe seems just so healthy. I think perhaps it's the pure, glassy appearance of the rice noodles and the lack of gluten which stops them congregating, pasta-style, in your tummy for hours after eating. Enjoyed all over East Asia and added as a staple to broths and stir-fries, they are my noodle of choice. The recipe does require quite a lot of chopping, but with a sharp knife you'll cut through it in no time. Putting it all together at the end is a cinch.

PREP TIME 15 MINUTES   SERVES 4   COOK TIME 2 MINUTES

150g vermicelli rice noodles

A drizzle of mild olive oil

300g large, cooked and peeled prawns

1 green apple, sliced paper-thin

180g sugarsnaps, each cut into 3 on the diagonal

3 tablespoons chopped mint

50g dry-roasted peanuts, roughly chopped

3 tablespoons chopped coriander or Thai basil, plus
    a little extra to garnish

Juice of 2 limes

2 tablespoons fish sauce

1 teaspoon caster sugar

1 Dunk the noodles into a pan full of boiling water and cook for 1½ minutes so they have softened but not overcooked – they will continue to soften once they are in the salad. Drain and cool under cold running water. Transfer to a large bowl and drizzle over a little olive oil to stop the strands sticking together.

2 Here is the easy bit: simply add all of the other ingredients (holding back a cluster of peanuts), and combine so everything is evenly distributed. Serve straight away with the reserved peanuts and extra chopped coriander or Thai basil resting on top.

DRUNKEN MUSSELS
WITH CIDER, LEEKS & CHORIZO

There is something satisfying about discovering a blanket of mussels clinging to a rock, plucking them from their home and then dropping them in the sink for a bath – though, of course, the supermarket is an easier way to acquire the shellfish! Mussels are at their juiciest during the first and last three months of the year, so pick your moment, savour the preparation and inhale the sea steam as the cooking begins.

PREP TIME 20 MINUTES   SERVES 2   COOK TIME 15 MINUTES

500g fresh mussels

2 tablespoons mild olive oil

30g butter

100g raw chorizo, sliced into thin rounds

2 garlic cloves, peeled and finely chopped

2 medium leeks, finely sliced into rounds

A cluster of thyme sprigs

400ml cider

3 tablespoons double cream

Plenty of freshly chopped flat-leaf parsley

Bread, to serve

1 First prepare the mussels. Scrub them to remove any sand or beards, knocking away any barnacles if you discover them. Discard any open mussels that refuse to close even when given a sharp tap. Rinse well under cold water and set aside.

2 Heat the olive oil and butter in a large saucepan over a medium heat and sauté the chorizo. Fry for a few minutes until you have a rust-coloured bubbling larva at the bottom of the pot. Add the garlic, leeks and thyme and cook for a further few minutes, until the leeks begin to soften and lose their shape.

3 Turn up the heat and add the cider and mussels. Cover tightly with a lid and steam for 5–7 minutes, shaking the pan once or twice to encourage the mussels to open. Reduce the heat to a simmer and, using a large slotted spoon, remove the mussels to deep warmed bowls, again discarding any that have not opened.

4 Pour the cream into the juices and cook for a further couple of minutes before dredging your waiting mussels. Sprinkle parsley liberally on top and serve with a chunk of bread to mop up the juices.

TOMATO, ANCHOVY
& GARLIC SPAGHETTI

Most of us have been victims of 'summer jobs' in school holidays. My pennies (literally) were earned tending to the neighbours' dogs, vegetables or post while they were holidaying. One occupation that cropped up many times over was looking after Mr Pask's tomatoes. He had a tiny greenhouse that became stiflingly sweaty in the summer sun and was packed with tomato plants dripping with fruit. Years later I only think a tomato is really good if it smells like that greenhouse, dusty with scent, and is deep red in colour.

PREP TIME 15 MINUTES   SERVES 4   COOK TIME 20 MINUTES

4 tablespoons olive oil

4 large garlic cloves, peeled and finely chopped

1 teaspoon dried chilli flakes

650g fresh tomatoes, roughly chopped

500ml hot vegetable stock

400g angel spaghetti

125g fresh anchovy fillets in olive oil, drained
   and roughly chopped, or kept whole if you prefer

A handful of basil leaves, roughly chopped (reserve a few
   whole leaves for garnish)

Sea salt and freshly ground black pepper

1 Heat the oil over a medium heat in the bottom of a large, deep saucepan. Add the garlic and chilli flakes and cook until the smell is released, about 1 minute.

2 Add the chopped tomatoes (stand back to avoid the spitting!) and turn the heat down to low. Cook, covered, for 8–10 minutes, stirring half way through. By this stage almost all the tomatoes should have broken down. Season with a generous pinch of salt and plenty of freshly ground black pepper.

3 Pour the vegetable stock into the pan, bring to a simmer then reduce the heat to low. Add the spaghetti and cook, covered, for 5–6 minutes, giving everything a good stir half way through.

4 Stir in three-quarters of the anchovy fillets and the chopped basil until all is beautifully combined. You should add a touch more stock here if you feel it's needed.

5 Serve immediately, with a basil leaf and the remaining anchovies balancing on top.

PRAWN, ARTICHOKE
& LEMON RISOTTO

One bag of risotto rice can rescue you from many a tricky culinary situation: it can become creamy rice pudding to be eaten with an immense dollop of home-made strawberry jam, risotto cakes branded crispy from a second frying or, as we have here, it can be cooked with garlic, hot stock and punchy ingredients. The three keys to a risotto's success are: a chef with the patience of a bird watcher, ingredients that scream quality and guests who are ready! Unlike bird watchers, risotto is decidedly impatient and doesn't like to be kept waiting.

PREP TIME 10 MINUTES   SERVES 4   COOK TIME 25 MINUTES

2 tablespoons olive oil

1 onion, finely chopped

2 garlic cloves, peeled and finely chopped

½ teaspoon fennel seeds

350g Arborio or Carnaroli risotto rice

200ml dry white wine

1–1.2 litres piping-hot vegetable stock

250g raw king prawns, peeled and deveined but with the tails still attached

Grated zest and juice of 1 lemon

8 chargrilled artichoke hearts, quartered

4 tablespoons finely grated Parmesan cheese

Sea salt and freshly ground black pepper

TO SERVE

Sprigs of fresh dill

Grated Parmesan cheese

A drizzle of extra virgin olive oil

1 Heat the olive oil in a deep sauté pan over a low heat. Cook the chopped onion for about 5 minutes, until it is soft but not coloured. Add the garlic and fennel seeds and continue to cook for 1 more minute.

2 Over a gentle heat, add the risotto rice to the pan and stir so the grains are coated in oil. Add the white wine and stir until absorbed. Gradually add the stock, one ladleful at a time, stirring each one until it's absorbed before adding the next. The amount of stock you add should become smaller when the rice is nearly done – this is a delicate process! Season.

3 When the risotto is al dente and the pan isn't dry, add the prawns, and lemon zest and juice. Cook for a further 2–3 minutes until the prawns have turned a rosy-cheek pink. Have a taste and see if the seasoning is correct – if not, this is your moment. Stir in the artichoke hearts and Parmesan until warmed through.

4 Finally, make sure the consistency is correct: risotto shouldn't hold its shape; instead it should slowly crawl to the edge of the plate on which it is served. Add a little more hot stock if you think the finished dish could be a little looser. Serve with a sprig of fresh dill and a drizzle of olive oil, plus some extra Parmesan for the table.

SLOW-COOKED SQUID
WITH CHORIZO & BEANS

Flash-frying squid may be the most familiar method of cooking this ocean delicacy, but here is a slow-cooked alternative. The squid seemingly tenses after initial cooking, though quickly relaxes into the pot after a longer soak in its bath of wine. A mellow flavour complements the fiery chorizo and herbed, juicy beans that I hope you will enjoy.

PREP TIME 15 MINUTES   SERVES 4   COOK TIME 1 HOUR

1 tablespoon olive oil

150g raw chorizo, cut into 1cm rounds

1 large red onion, finely sliced

3 garlic cloves, peeled and finely chopped

1 large fresh red chilli, deseeded and finely sliced

2 large plum tomatoes, each cut into 8 wedges

200ml sweet white wine

150ml hot chicken stock

1 bouquet garni, made up of 2 fresh bay leaves, 2–3 flat-leaf parsley stalks (reserve the leaves for the garnish) and a cluster of fresh thyme

400g cleaned squid tubes, sliced into 1cm rings (keep the tentacles if you are able)

1 x 400g tin flageolet beans, drained and rinsed

Sea salt and freshly ground black pepper

1 Heat the oil in a large casserole over a high heat. Add the chorizo and fry until it begins to crisp, has coloured at the edges and has filled the kitchen with its scent.

2 Remove the chorizo from the pan using a slotted spoon and add the onion to the oil left behind. Reduce the heat to medium and sauté the onion for a couple of minutes before adding the garlic and chilli. Continue to heat for 2–3 minutes until both the onion and garlic are soft.

3 Stir through the tomato wedges and cook until they have begun to loose their shape, about 2 minutes. Pour in the white wine and reduce by half, allowing the alcohol to boil off.

4 Stir in the stock, then return the chorizo to the pot along with the bouquet garni and the squid rings. Simmer gently, covered, for 30 minutes. Add the flageolet beans and cook, uncovered, for a final 20 minutes.

5 Serve garnished with the reserved parsley leaves and a good grinding of salt and pepper.

FISH BROTH

WITH NEW POTATOES & FRESH GREEN PESTO

'You are what you eat' is a mantra we've all grown familiar with and I agree that cleansing food makes for a cleansed mind. This particular recipe, with its fresh fish poached in a wonderful hot broth, makes me feel virtuous whether I've run a '10K' or sat through a TV marathon. As is often the case, don't add the fish until the last possible moment to avoid overcooking it.

PREP TIME 15 MINUTES   SERVES 4   COOK TIME 25 MINUTES

2 red mullet fillets, skin on, cut into 3–5cm pieces

8 raw king prawns, with tails still attached

200g plaice or other white fish, cut into 3–5cm pieces

12 mussels, debearded and scrubbed

8 clams, scrubbed

2 teaspoons olive oil

1 large onion, chopped

2 garlic cloves, peeled and finely chopped

600g new potatoes, scrubbed and larger ones cut in half

100g fresh green pesto (the better quality, the better the dish)

250ml sweet white wine

1 litre hot fish stock

3 plum tomatoes, roughly diced

60g watercress, roughly chopped

Crusty loaf, to serve

1 Prepare your fish and have it sitting calmly on a plate in the fridge ready for the final step. The minutes pass more quickly than you think and it's good to be prepared.

2 Heat the oil in a large saucepan over a medium heat. Fry the onion for a couple of minutes until it begins to soften, then add the garlic. Continue to fry until the onion has cooked, but be careful not to let it colour.

3 Add the potatoes and pesto and stir to combine. Pour over the white wine and fish stock and bring to the boil. Reduce the heat and simmer for 15 minutes until the

potatoes are almost tender. Add the tomatoes and continue to simmer for 5 minutes. (Pop some bread in the oven so you can serve the fish with a warm, crusty loaf.)

4 This is the last step and should be done when your guests are already sitting at the table. Add the fish, shellfish and watercress to the pot and cook, covered, for 2–3 minutes until the mussels and clams have opened and the fish has turned opaque.

5 Ladle into bowls and serve immediately. Don't let that fish overcook!

 TIP – I'D RECOMMEND HAVING A LARGE BOWL OF WARM WATER ON THE TABLE WITH A SLICE OF LEMON OR TWO. THAT WAY YOUR GUESTS CAN RINSE THEIR FINGERS AFTER PEELING THE PRAWNS AND SHELLING THE MUSSELS.

ALL-IN-ONE FISH PIE

Fish pie is the edible equivalent of a robust bear hug but oh my, making the traditional dish is a little more time consuming. However, this one-pot fish pie has had a makeover. It relies on a few minor tweaks and tricks making it absolutely scrumptious, ready within the hour and with minimal washing up.

PREP TIME 15 MINUTES	SERVES 6	COOK TIME 30 MINUTES

Olive oil, for greasing

250g pollock fillets, skinned and cut into delicate 2–3cm chunks

250g salmon, skinned and cut into delicate 2–3cm chunks

250g smoked haddock, skinned and cut into delicate 2–3cm chunks

2 tablespoons plain flour

1 red onion, very finely sliced

2 carrots (approx. 200g), peeled and coarsely grated

150g frozen peas (no need to pre-cook them)

500ml good-quality, shop-bought white sauce, or homemade if you have the time

A good clump of dill, roughly chopped

Grated zest of 1 lemon

150g filo pastry

50g butter, melted

Sea salt and freshly ground black pepper

1 Preheat the oven to 180°C/gas mark 4. Lightly grease a 1.5–2-litre ovenproof dish with a little olive oil.

2 Put the fish chunks in a large bowl and sprinkle over the plain flour. Gently toss so each piece of fish is lightly coated. Add the vegetables, white sauce, dill (reserving a little for the garnish) and lemon zest. Gently combine so that the sauce is spread throughout the mixture. Season and transfer to the ovenproof dish.

3 Brush one side of the filo pastry sheets with butter and then scrunch up, leaving the buttered side facing upwards. Place on top of the fish mixture. There is no need to be too neat; the more abstract, the more beautiful, in my opinion. Give a good twist of black pepper, a sprinkling of salt and a little dusting of the reserved dill.

4 Bake in the oven for 30–35 minutes, until the pastry is golden on top and the sauce is bubbling below. Remove from the oven and allow the fish to continue cooking for 5 minutes or so before serving.

 TIP – IF YOU HAVE A FEROCIOUS OVEN AND YOUR FILO LOOKS TO BE BROWNING TOO QUICKLY, COVER WITH A LITTLE FOIL FOR THE LAST FEW MINUTES OF COOKING.

CLUCKY
& GAME

Winter 2011 was spent living in Zimbabwe on a chicken farm. I didn't visit the birds every day but as I approached their houses a musty, organic smell swept through the shiny wire and I was fully aware I'd left London smog behind.

Life for the chickens began in a hatchery where eggs were cautiously warmed and turned until the chicks were ready to fracture their fragile houses. The babies burst forth, tiny and bare-bodied, nobly fighting for survival to make it through their first hours. With every day the chicks grew stronger on our African soil, breathing in the sun, inhaling their feed and scrabbling in red dust. My neighbours seemed happy.

Our house rations proffered three chickens a week so it was during these months I became more speedy at jointing a chicken then ever before. We played with roasting, steaming, pot roasting, poaching and frying. You name it, we tried it. Within this chapter are both chicken and game recipes that have been given a seal of approval and have been tested with both African and English meats.

CHICKEN & SAUSAGE
CASSOULET

Forget those tinned concoctions of baked beans and rubbery frankfurters. Yes, the traditional French cassoulet does require some preparation, but once you're over the initial effort you can just sit back and let the flavours develop and mingle. It really is worth every minute. *Bon appétit.*

PREP TIME 1 HOUR (PLUS OVERNIGHT SOAKING)   **SERVES 8**   COOK TIME 2½ HOURS

500g dried haricot or cannellini beans

2 tablespoons olive oil

6 free-range chicken drumsticks, skin on

4 free-range chicken thighs, skin on

6 Toulouse sausages

200g bacon, cut into dice

2 onions, cut in half

12 cloves

2 carrots, scrubbed clean and cut in half widthways

4 garlic cloves, peeled and left whole

2 sticks of celery, each sliced into 5

2 fresh bay leaves

4–5 sprigs of thyme

1 tablespoon tomato purée

Sea salt and freshly ground black pepper

1 The night before you want to cook, put the beans into a large bowl and cover with cold water. Allow to soak overnight, then drain and put in a large, heavy-bottomed casserole with a capacity of about 6 litres. Cover the beans with fresh water and bring to a rolling boil for 10 minutes, then drain again and set the softened beans aside.

2 Heat the olive oil in the casserole and set about browning the chicken, sausages and bacon. This will have to be done in batches so that the meat browns rather than steams; the rule of thumb is that there should be 1cm space around each piece of meat. Cut the sausages in half, then cover all the meat and set aside.

3 Wipe the pot clean and add the soaked beans. Stud each onion half with 3 cloves and add them to the pot along with the carrots, garlic, celery, bay leaves and a sprig or two of thyme. Top up with approximately 1.5 litres fresh water, then cover, bring to a simmer and gently cook for an hour. The beans will still be quite firm at this stage.

4 Preheat the oven to 180°C/gas mark 4.

5 Remove the studded onion halves and discard. Add the browned meat to the pot and gently stir in. Add the tomato purée and a few more thyme sprigs. Season the dish more than you think you need and pop it in the oven. Cook, covered, for 1½ hours. Check occasionally to make sure that the cassoulet isn't drying out – add hot water if needed.

6 Remove any unwieldy thyme sprigs just before serving and give the whole thing a stir. You've done it and, my goodness, doesn't it smell good?

POT-ROAST CHICKEN
WITH NEW POTATOES & SPINACH

A one-pot recipe book without a pot-roast chicken would be like Christmas Day without a turkey, and there's a reason why this recipe, in particular, became a staple Italian meal. Once you've made the stuffing it's a throw-it-all-in affair that can be a lifesaver when preparing a busy Sunday lunch.

PREP TIME 20 MINUTES · SERVES 6 · COOK TIME 1 HOUR 20 MINUTES

100g fresh, fine breadcrumbs

2 garlic cloves, peeled and crushed

3 tablespoons good-quality basil pesto

½ nutmeg, grated, or 1 teaspoon ground nutmeg

3 tablespoons chopped flat-leaf parsley

1 free-range egg, beaten

1 whole free-range chicken (1.2–1.4kg)

1 tablespoon vegetable oil

1 onion, peeled and cut into wedges

2 fresh bay leaves

3 sticks of celery, cut into 2cm chunks

1kg baby new potatoes, scrubbed, large ones cut in half

1 litre hot chicken stock

260g bag of spinach

Sea salt and freshly ground black pepper

You will also need a 30cm length of kitchen string or a few wooden cocktail sticks.

1 Make the stuffing by mixing together the breadcrumbs, garlic, pesto, nutmeg and 2 tablespoons of the parsley with the egg. Ram into the cavity of the chicken and, using the kitchen string or cocktail sticks, do your best to close the opening completely.

2 Rub the chicken with salt and pepper. Heat the oil in the bottom of a large casserole and, using tongs to help you, brown the chicken on all sides. As my mother would say, resist the urge to keep moving the chicken. Allow each side to brown before turning to another.

3 Turn down the heat. Add the onion wedges, bay leaves, celery and potatoes around the chicken and pour in the stock. Bring the whole lot to the boil, cover and reduce to a simmer for 1 hour or until your chicken is cooked – test that the juices run clear.

4 Take the chicken out of the pot (a word of warning… wear an apron to avoid being splattered) and set aside to cool slightly. Meanwhile, add the spinach and remaining parsley to the broth and allow to wilt. Squish the potatoes slightly if you would like the sauce to thicken up.

5 Cut the chicken into serving portions (I find kitchen scissors the best for this), then remove the stuffing and slice it into six. Spoon the vegetables into shallow bowls and top each with a chicken portion and a slice of stuffing.

PEPPERED CHICKEN
THIGHS WITH SAGE, HAZELNUTS & NEW POTATOES

Soft green peppercorns are a beautiful addition to this dish. They are gently spiced, more delicate than their black cousins, and are now available in most supermarkets, sold in jars of brine. Here I've simmered them with whole hazelnuts and Charlotte potatoes to make an appealing backdrop to tender poultry thighs.

PREP TIME 15 MINUTES   SERVES 6   COOK TIME 45 MINUTES

12 free-range chicken thighs, with bones and skin

Olive oil, for rubbing onto the thighs

3 red onions, each cut into 8–10 wedges

750g Charlotte potatoes (or any small waxy potato), halved lengthways

4 garlic cloves, peeled and chopped

1 teaspoon mustard powder

1 tablespoon soft green peppercorns in brine, roughly chopped

2 x 400g tins chopped tomatoes

400ml hot chicken stock

100g whole hazelnuts

½ bunch sage leaves (approx. 40g)

1 Preheat the oven to 180°C/gas mark 4.

2 Heat an ovenproof casserole over a medium heat. Rub the chicken thighs with olive oil and fry until golden. I'd do this three at a time to avoid overcrowding your pot. Set the golden thighs aside and continue until all have been seen to. Pour away some of the excess fat that might have escaped from the thighs – you just need enough left to fry the onions.

3 Add the onions and fry for a couple of minutes before adding the potatoes. Fry for 6–8 minutes until the vegetables begin to crisp. Add the garlic, mustard powder and peppercorns and continue to fry for a further couple of minutes.

4 Toss in the tomatoes, stock, hazelnuts and 12 or so sage leaves, roughly chopped. Return the chicken thighs to the pot, sitting on top of the vegetables, pop the casserole in the oven and cook, covered, for 30 minutes, followed by 15 minutes with the lid off.

5 When the potatoes are tender and the chicken is cooked through, remove from the oven. Scatter with one or two chopped sage leaves just before serving. Perfect.

PEANUT
CURRIED CHICKEN

We are born knowing that some ingredients belong together: pork and apples, strawberries and cream, eggs and bacon. Others happen upon us later in life and we wish we'd discovered them earlier. May I present sweet potatoes and peanut butter! The potatoes break down during cooking leaving the chicken with a deliciously sweet, thick sauce. Go on, I dare you.

PREP TIME 20 MINUTES　　　　　　　　SERVES 6　　　　　　　　COOK TIME 40 MINUTES

1 tablespoon vegetable oil

12 skinless, boneless, free-range chicken thighs, kept whole

1 tablespoon butter

2 large red onions, finely sliced

3 garlic cloves, peeled and sliced

1 teaspoon dried chilli flakes

3 heaped tablespoons organic crunchy peanut butter

1 tablespoon mild curry paste or 1 teaspoon mild curry powder

1 tablespoon tomato purée

800g chunky sweet potatoes, peeled and cut into 3cm cubes

400ml coconut milk

½ bunch coriander, chopped

Sea salt and freshly ground black pepper

1 Heat the oil in the bottom of a heavy saucepan. Fry the chicken thighs in batches until each is just beginning to turn golden; this should take a few minutes on each side. Set the chicken aside, covered, while you crack on with the base of the recipe.

2 Melt the butter in the saucepan and add the onion, garlic and chilli flakes. Fry over a medium heat for a couple of minutes until soft and steamy but not coloured. Stir through the peanut butter, curry paste and tomato purée and heat for a further minute. Ensure that all the ingredients are nicely incorporated.

3 Add the sweet potatoes, pour over the coconut milk and give everything a good stir. The coconut milk should reach roughly half way up the pan, and don't worry that it doesn't cover the sweet potatoes. Bring to the boil and reduce the heat to medium. Cover and allow the potatoes to simmer for 10 minutes.

4 Return the seared chicken thighs to the pot and continue to simmer for another 15 minutes until the meat is thoroughly cooked through. Season as you wish. Just before serving, stir a good clump of chopped coriander through the pot.

 TIP - IF YOU SUDDENLY DISCOVER THAT YOU ARE OUT OF COCONUT MILK, USE 350ML SEMI-SKIMMED MILK AND 50ML DOUBLE CREAM FOR A SLIGHTLY DIFFERENT VERSION OF THIS DISH.

OOZY OVEN-BAKED RICE
WITH TENDER CHICKEN

This recipe is stacked with flavour and has become a Fuggle staple, one of my autumnal top ten. My recommendation is to use paella rice, but risotto rice is fine too – both make for a deliciously gloopy accompaniment to the tender chicken legs.

PREP TIME 15 MINUTES   SERVES 4   COOK TIME 45–50 MINUTES

4 free-range chicken legs, skin on

1 tablespoon olive oil

1 large onion, roughly chopped

200g smoked streaky bacon rashers, cut into
   2cm pieces

400g chestnut mushrooms, finely sliced

200g paella rice

800ml hot chicken stock

3 garlic cloves, peeled and finely chopped

4 tablespooons chopped flat-leaf parsley

1 Preheat the oven to 170°C/gas mark 3.

2 In a large ovenproof, heavy-based saucepan, fry the chicken legs in the oil until crispy and golden. Remove from the pot and set aside.

3 Fry the onion in the same saucepan for a minute or so until it begins to soften. Add the bacon and continue to fry at a high heat. Stir occasionally until the bacon is cooked through, then throw in the chestnut mushrooms to cook for 2–3 minutes. The mushrooms don't need to be crispy; they will cook thoroughly in the oven and it's lovely to have the juices running into the rice.

4 Stir through the paella rice, stock, garlic and half of the parsley. Season. Nestle the reserved chicken legs in the surface. Pop the lid on and bake in the oven for 45–50 minutes or until the rice is lovely and tender. If you are in the kitchen, give the pot a stir half way through the cooking time; it's not essential but it does prevent anything from sticking to the base.

5 Remove the pot from the oven and unveil your dinner. Garnish with the rest of the parsley and serve with a green salad, if you wish.

SPANISH CHICKEN
WITH CHORIZO & GARLIC

Years ago I spent a month winding around the railways of Spain, stopping where the guidebooks spoke of traditional plazas, museums and fine Spanish cuisine. My memory holds Seville in particular esteem. It must have been to do with the heavily laden orange trees and a supper eaten while watching university students pour out of the library at the most ungodly of hours. I remember eating something similar to this dish and have tried to re-create it, as closely as scribbled notes written by candlelight will allow. *Ole!*

PREP TIME 20 MINUTES   SERVES 6   COOK TIME 1 HOUR

1 tablespoon olive oil

6 large free-range chicken thighs, with bones and skin

200g chorizo, cut into 1–2cm chunks

1 onion, peeled and cut into thin wedges

2 medium leeks, chopped into 2–3cm pieces

1 teaspoon Spanish smoked paprika (unsmoked is fine, too)

A pinch of dried saffron

2 whole heads of garlic, cut in half horizontally and left unpeeled

4 sprigs of thyme

200ml sweet white wine

250ml hot chicken stock

2 x 400g tins organic butter beans, drained and rinsed

Sea salt and freshly ground black pepper

1 Heat the olive oil in a large casserole until smoking hot. Fry the chicken legs on both sides until they are crisp and golden, then transfer to a waiting plate. Keep the heat on high and add the chorizo chunks to the pot. Fry for a minute on each side and remove from the casserole with a slotted spoon so as to leave their oil behind.

2 Add the onion, leeks and smoked paprika and fry in the delicious chorizo oil. Reduce the heat, cover and soften the vegetables for 3–4 minutes, but check that they don't catch on the bottom of the pot.

3 Add the saffron, garlic halves, thyme, wine and chicken stock to the pot along with the chicken and chorizo. Season well, cover and simmer over a medium heat for 30 minutes. Let the pot do the work; yours is almost done.

4 Stir in the butter beans and cook for a further 10 minutes before serving with a baked potato or two.

LIME ROASTED CHICKEN
WITH POTATOES

Sundays all over the country signal roast-chicken lunches and copious platefuls of spuds, but it's easily forgotten that these roasts require an impressive degree of skill – not least managing all the timings and coping with the hungry anticipation. All that juggling may drive you to this wonderfully simple, all-in-one method. You might just have enough time to warm your plates!

PREP TIME 15 MINUTES	SERVES 4	COOK TIME 1 HOUR 20 MINUTES

1.5kg free-range chicken

2 whole heads of garlic, cut in half horizontally

800g red-skinned potatoes, washed and halved

3 tablespoons mild-tasting olive oil

3 limes, zested and halved

3 plump fresh red chillies, thinly sliced on the diagonal

2 large red onions, each cut into 8 wedges

Sea salt and freshly ground black pepper

1 Preheat the oven to 200°C/gas mark 6.

2 Season the cavity of the chicken well and stuff with half a garlic head. Rub the halved potatoes with 1 tablespoon of the olive oil. Use your hands to give them a good coating. Place in a large roasting tin and nestle the chicken in the centre. Rub a further glug of oil over the chicken and season the skin generously.

3 Place the chicken and potatoes in the centre of the oven. After 30 minutes, remove from the oven and reduce the temperature to 180°C/gas mark 4.

4 Add all the remaining ingredients to the nest around the chicken and sprinkle over the lime zest. Give the limes a good squeeze over the potatoes (leave the squeezed halves amongst the potatoes – they look wonderful and will only add flavour) and roast for a further 45 minutes or until the chicken juices run clear.

5 Transfer the chicken to a carving board and allow the meat to rest for 10 minutes. Carve and serve with your delicious crusty potatoes and a bowl or two of vegetables.

 TIP – MAKE THE GRAVY IN THE VERY SAME TIN THAT YOU USED TO ROAST THE CHICKEN. SIMPLY REMOVE EVERYTHING THEN TRANSFER THE TIN TO THE HOB AND PLACE DIRECTLY ON A VERY LOW HEAT. SPRINKLE 2 TABLESPOONS OF PLAIN FLOUR OVER THE DELICIOUS CHICKEN JUICES AND STIR UNTIL YOU HAVE A THICK PASTE. VERY GENTLY, ADD 500ML HOT CHICKEN STOCK, MIXING WELL AFTER EACH ADDITION. SEASON AND ADD A SPOT OF MUSTARD SHOULD YOU FEEL THE GRAVY NEEDS IT. THAT'S IT – DONE!

CHICKEN POT PIE

There are few dishes that aren't lifted by a lid of pastry and chicken stew is no exception. The good news is that there's no rubbing of butter into flour as I've cheated and bought my pastry from a shop (well, at least you're going to make your own sumptuous filling).

PREP TIME 20 MINUTES   SERVES 6   COOK TIME 45 MINUTES

500g block of puff pastry

50g butter

250g chestnut mushrooms, thinly sliced

3 medium leeks, thinly sliced

3 garlic cloves, peeled and finely chopped

700g free-range chicken breasts, cut into
     bite-sized chunks

1 tablespoon finely chopped tarragon

15g soft green peppercorns in brine, roughly chopped

3 tablespoons plain flour

300ml hot chicken stock

1 free-range egg yolk, beaten

Sea salt and freshly ground black pepper

1 The first step is to roll out the puff pastry on a lightly floured surface until approximately 5mm thick. Using a sharp knife, cut around a 2-litre, ovenproof pan to create a circle of pastry that will become the lid to your pie. Slide the pastry onto a plate and leave to rest in the fridge while the filling is made.

2 Preheat the oven to 200°C/gas mark 6.

3 Heat half the butter in your chosen pot and fry off the mushrooms until they begin to crisp and have lost lots of their moisture. Set aside and add the remaining butter to the pan. Add the leeks and garlic and gently fry until soft. Take your time doing this; the leeks shouldn't colour at all.

4 Add the chicken pieces to the leeks and fry for 6–8 minutes so they start to cook. Your pan will be full to the brim, but that is a good thing! Return the mushrooms to the pan along with the tarragon and green peppercorns and sprinkle over the flour. Pour over the chicken stock, give everything a good stir to combine, and bring to a simmer. Season to taste.

5 Remove the pan from the heat and place the puff pastry circle over the top, tucking the edges into the pot slightly. Decorate as you wish, traditionally with leaves, or why not go crazy? A pastry chicken could be fun. Use a little beaten egg to stick the decorations on. Make a small hole in the centre of the circle so the steam can escape and, working quickly, brush the whole lid with beaten egg.

6 Bake in the oven for 30 minutes or until the pastry is golden and crisp on top.

CHUBBY CHICKEN LEGS
WITH OLIVES, WHITE WINE & CAPERS

A deceptively simple dish to put together that makes an ideal supper for friends. There is something very comforting about dipping warm bread into juices and sponging up a messy plate – though perhaps you should really only do it in front of those you know very well. My suggestion would be to serve this with a hunk of bread and a glass of chilled white wine.

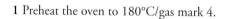

PREP TIME 10 MINUTES   SERVES 4   COOK TIME 40 MINUTES

3 tablespoons olive oil

75ml dry white wine

2 large garlic cloves, peeled and very finely sliced

100g Parmesan cheese, finely grated

4 plump free-range chicken legs, skin on

4 tomatoes, halved

A handful of black olives (approx. 125g)

2 tablespoons caper berries

Fresh bread, to serve

1 Preheat the oven to 180°C/gas mark 4.

2 Put the olive oil, white wine, garlic and half the Parmesan into a 2-litre ovenproof dish and stir vigorously to combine. Add the chicken legs and coat well with the sauce. Add the tomatoes, olives and capers to the dish and toss.

3 Turn the chicken so the plump side is facing up and sprinkle with Parmesan to cover, as if with a sheet of snow. Reserve a little of the Parmesan for sprinkling over the finished dish. Cook in the oven for 35–40 minutes, until the chicken meat is pulling away from the bone.

4 Give a final dusting of Parmesan and serve with hunks of bread.

SLOW-COOKED
QUAIL WITH WHEATBERRIES & BAY

Given that quail sits so beautifully with barley or spelt, it is only a small step further to partner it with wheatberries, a relatively new ingredient to cross our paths but one that I hope may become more familiar; it is available at good supermarkets. When cooked, wheatberries have a subtle, creamy, soft texture with a delicate, nutty taste that complements gamey quail flesh. Feel free to enjoy this one pot heated up after a long, chilly walk on the moors. The countryside seasons it wonderfully.

PREP TIME 20 MINUTES — SERVES 4 — COOK TIME 1 HOUR

3 tablespoons mild-tasting olive oil

4 quail

2 red onions, sliced into thin wedges

2 garlic cloves, peeled and sliced

2 carrots, scrubbed and roughly chopped

2 sticks of celery, finely chopped

1 heaped tablespoon tomato purée

200g wheatberries (or use pearl barley instead)

2 fresh bay leaves

1 generous sprig of thyme

300ml medium-bodied red wine

650ml fresh chicken stock

A little extra olive oil, for drizzling

Sea salt and freshly ground black pepper

1 Heat a glug of the olive oil in the bottom of a heavy-based saucepan over a medium heat and braise the little quail until they have taken on some colour. Set them aside, wrapped in foil.

2 Heat the remaining oil in the same pan, then add the onions, garlic and a small pinch of salt and stir for about 5 minutes. Add the carrots, celery and tomato purée and stir well to combine. Once the vegetables have softened, add the wheatberries, bay and thyme.

3 Pour over the wine and half of the chicken stock. Return the quail to the pot and nestle in amongst everything. Raise the heat slightly to a gentle simmer, then cook, uncovered, for about 30 minutes, stirring every now and then. Add more stock as you need, allowing the wheatberries to absorb the liquid before adding any more.

4 When the wheatberries are nutty and just tender, season well with salt, as they will need it. Stir in a little more olive oil just before serving.

THE FAMOUS

COQ AU VIN

A sociable dish in all regards. Chicken, salty bacon, garlic, nutty mushrooms and a healthy carafe of wine, left to get to know each other over hours on a hot stove – it's little wonder that this combination has made history. Throw in the ingredients and then let the pot perform the introductions. For the best results, marinate the chicken overnight. Serve with some buttered mash or a hunk of home-made garlic bread.

PREP TIME 20 MINUTES (PLUS OVERNIGHT MARINATING)

SERVES 4–6

COOK TIME 1½ HOURS

4 free-range chicken drumsticks and 4 thighs, with bones and skin

600ml full-bodied red wine

75ml brandy

1 bouquet garni (1 sprig of fresh thyme, 1 bay leaf and 2 fresh sprigs of flat-leaf parsley, tied together with a piece of kitchen string)

2 tablespoons vegetable oil

200g bacon lardons or streaky bacon, chopped

12 shallots, peeled and left whole

250g chestnut mushrooms, sliced

3 sticks of celery, sliced into 2.5cm pieces

3 garlic cloves, peeled and sliced

2 tablespoons plain flour

Sea salt and freshly ground black pepper

Fresh flat-leaf parsley, to garnish

1 Put the chicken into a large bowl and pour over the wine and brandy. Nestle in the bouquet garni, cover and leave to soak overnight in the fridge.

2 Heat 1 tablespoon of the oil in an ovenproof casserole and crisp up the bacon until golden. Lift out of the pot and into a bowl, leaving the fat behind.

3 Next up is the chicken. Remove the chicken from the marinade and pat dry – this will make the skin far easier to brown and will prevent angry oil spitting. If needed, pour a little more oil into the pan and, over a medium heat, fry the chicken pieces until the skin is a pale gold. You may have to do this in batches. Set the chicken aside with the lardons. There will be a deliciously sticky layer clinging to the bottom of the pan, which will provide stacks of flavour so don't be tempted to clean it.

4 Add the remaining oil to the pot and brown the shallots for a minute before adding the mushrooms, celery and garlic and frying everything for a good 5 minutes. Return the chicken and bacon and sprinkle over the flour. Add the bouquet garni and pour over the marinating liquid. Season with oodles of salt and pepper.

5 Bring to the boil, cover and simmer gently for 1 hour until the chicken is cooked through. Garnish with parsley and serve.

DUCK
WITH REDCURRANTS, PLUMS & PUY LENTILS

Duck boasts an impressively decadent flavour, and I've succumbed to this aura by pairing the breasts with port, plums and lentils… because nothing else would do.

PREP TIME 15 MINUTES   SERVES 2   COOK TIME 30 MINUTES

1 tablespoon cornflour

A good bundle of thyme (about 10 sprigs)

200ml port

100ml hot vegetable stock

2 garlic cloves, peeled and very finely sliced

4 red plums, stoned and cut in half

300g Puy lentils, cooked (you can buy these in tins)

2 duck breast fillets

2 tablespoons redcurrant jelly

Sea salt and freshly ground black pepper

1 Preheat the oven to 200°C/gas mark 6.

2 First things first: pop the cornflour in a small glass and add approximately 1 tablespoon of water. Stir until you have a smooth paste and set aside.

3 Scatter the thyme sprigs over the base of a small roasting tin to form a mattress for the duck. Pour over the port, vegetable stock and cornflour paste and give a gentle stir. Nestle the garlic slices, plums and Puy lentils in the tin and cook in the oven for 12–15 minutes, until the plums have begun to wilt.

4 Meanwhile, rinse the duck fillets under cold running water and pat them dry using kitchen paper. Using a sharp knife, make several diagonal slices into the skin, taking

care not to slice the meat. Rub the redcurrant jelly into the skin and season well with salt and pepper. Lay the duck breasts over the plums and lentils, skin-side up, making sure that the skin is not submerged in the liquid. Bake in the oven for 15 minutes.

5 While the duck is cooking, preheat the grill to high. (If your oven and grill are combined, wait until the 15 minutes are up then cover the duck in foil so that it keeps warm while the grill heats up.) Place the duck under the grill for 4–5 minutes – this will give you lovely crispy skin.

6 Allow the duck to sit for a short while, then slice it and serve atop a hill of plums and lentils.

BRAISED DUCK LEGS
WITH JUNIPER & GINGER

We buy chicken legs without too much thought, but duck legs, for no good reason, seem a little more daunting. This intimidation is an urban myth, an old wives' tale and a conspiracy theory all rolled into one. You'll find below one of the easiest recipes in the whole book – seriously, it can be prepared in moments and then the hard work is left to the oven. I've served the finished dish in a number of ways, so put your own stamp on the recipe and choose if you'd like it hot or cold, in a sandwich or heaped on a salad.

PREP TIME 10-15 MINUTES   SERVES 4   COOK TIME 2 HOURS

4 large carrots, scrubbed and chopped into
   roughly 1cm rounds
5 sticks of celery, chopped into 1cm cubes
2 large onions, roughly chopped
6 garlic cloves, peeled and finely sliced
6cm piece of fresh ginger, peeled and finely chopped
2 teaspoons juniper berries, finely chopped

A glug of vegetable oil
Grated zest and juice of 1 orange
4 duck legs, skin on
2 teaspoons za'atar (optional)
4–5 spring onions, chopped
Sea salt and freshly ground black pepper

1 Preheat the oven to 180°C/gas mark 4.

2 Put all the chopped vegetables, ginger and juniper berries in the bottom of a shallow casserole and drizzle with a good glug of vegetable oil and the orange juice. (Take a moment to smell the juniper berries and inhale your gin fix without the need for tonic.) Add the orange zest and toss everything thoroughly.

3 Lay the duck legs over the vegetables and season generously with salt and pepper. Sprinkle the za'atar over each leg. Now you've done the hard work, simply pop in

the oven, uncovered, for 1½–2 hours depending on the size of your duck legs. The dish is done when the flesh can be pulled away from the bone with the touch of a fork.

4 Take the pot out of the oven and admire your work. Allow to cool for a few minutes before removing the meat from the legs using two forks as a means of attack. Shred the flesh and skin and return to your pot.

5 Tumble everything together with the spring onions, check for seasoning, and serve as you like.

 TIP – ZA'ATAR IS A WONDERFUL SPICE MIX THAT INCLUDES OREGANO, MARJORAM, TOASTED SESAME SEEDS AND SALT. IT'S AVAILABLE AT MOST BIG SUPERMARKETS AND IS WORTH SEEKING OUT.

CREAMY RABBIT

WITH PLENTY OF HERBS

Yes, rabbits are very sweet and might prompt images of Benjamin Bunny, but they do taste extremely good. Make friends with a butcher so he can slip you the youngest, most tender pieces, which will taste a little more spritely than the grandparent. The meat is very lean, so you need to add a little fat when cooking, which helps to give some richness to the recipe.

PREP TIME 20 MINUTES   SERVES 4   COOK TIME 1¼ HOURS

1–2 tablespoons olive oil

700g diced rabbit

150g pancetta cubes

1 red onion, roughly chopped

200g celeriac, peeled and cut into 2cm chunks

1 x 400g tin good-quality plum tomatoes, each tomato squished with the back of a spoon or your clean hands

250ml hot vegetable stock

2 sprigs of thyme

1 large sprig of rosemary

2 fresh bay leaves

100ml double cream

100g Kalamata black olives

Fresh flat-leaf parsley, to garnish

1 Heat some of the oil in a pan over a high heat. Season the rabbit and fry in the pan so each piece takes on a golden tinge. Remove the meat and reduce the heat slightly. Add a little more oil to the pan and toss in the pancetta. Fry until just crispy, remove and set aside with the waiting rabbit.

2 Add the red onion to the pan and gently fry for 2–3 minutes, before adding the celeriac chunks and cooking for a further 3–4 minutes. Return the rabbit and pancetta to the pan, then add the tomatoes, stock and herbs. Top up with a little water if needed, so the rabbit is just covered in liquid.

3 Simmer, uncovered, for 45 minutes or until the rabbit is cooked through – older ones may take a little longer. Add the cream to the pot for the final 10 minutes.

4 Just before serving, run the olives through the dish and sprinkle with fresh parsley.

RABBIT POT
WITH MUSTARD & PISTACHIOS

Don't ignore tender rabbit meat when it comes to one pots: the flavour is not dissimilar to that of chicken but with a little more depth, and if you're lucky enough to be given a piece of saddle, the texture will leave you wanting more. The pistachios in this recipe are decadent but the green nuts taste and look beautiful – include them if you can.

PREP TIME 25 MINUTES   **SERVES 6**   COOK TIME 1 HOUR

2 rabbits, jointed

3 tablespoons plain flour

3 tablespoons mild-tasting olive oil

1 onion, roughly chopped

2 garlic cloves, peeled and finely sliced

300g turnips (about 4), peeled and cut into 2.5cm chunks

4 new-season carrots, scrubbed and cut into 2.5cm chunks

2 sprigs of rosemary

1 heaped tablespoon tomato purée

2 sprigs of tarragon, plus extra to serve

Zest of 1 lemon, peeled into lengths using a vegetable peeler

2 tablespooons Dijon mustard

300ml dry cider

300ml hot chicken stock

50g shelled pistachios, roughly chopped

1 Dust the rabbit joints with flour, shaking off any excess.

2 Heat 2 tablespoons of the oil in a large casserole over a high heat. Brown the rabbit pieces on all sides, then remove and set aside.

3 Reduce the heat slightly and add the remaining oil to the pot. Fry the onion gently for 5 minutes until it begins to soften. Add the garlic and any excess flour you have and cook for a further minute, stirring with a wooden spoon. Add the chunks of turnips and carrots and give them a good stir.

4 Return the rabbit to the pot with the rosemary, tarragon, lemon zest, mustard, cider, tomato purée and stock and slowly bring to the boil. Cover and simmer for 30 minutes, then remove the lid and cook for a further 30 minutes.

5 Remove from the heat and sprinkle over a good handful of chopped pistachios and some freshly chopped tarragon before serving. The splash of green will look stunning.

VENISON
& CHESTNUT POT

Sophisticated yet easy, this recipe has clambered into my easy dinner repertoire. I like the taste of venison, as it's gamey without being over the top, and wonderfully lean, so good for those who are keeping an eye on their cholesterol levels. My mother makes a lot of stews – it doesn't seem to matter if it's July or December – and so I've learnt to enjoy them all year round. Stews give a new lease of life to vegetables that might be lying sad and forgotten in the fridge, and they can also make a small amount of meat stretch to feed a big family. I know why she likes them.

PREP TIME 25 MINUTES · SERVES 4 · COOK TIME 2¼ HOURS

2 tablespoons vegetable oil

700g venison, cut into 3cm dice

2 medium onions, diced, or
   12 whole shallots, peeled

3 garlic cloves, peeled and sliced

3 tablespoons plain flour

2 medium carrots, peeled and cut into 2cm chunks

1 small swede, peeled and cut into 2–3cm cubes

1 or 2 sprigs of thyme

1 or 2 bay leaves

250ml full-bodied red wine

500ml good-quality beef stock

250g cooked and peeled chestnuts

2 tablespoons cranberry sauce (or redcurrant jelly
   if it's the wrong time of year)

Fresh flat-leaf parsley, to garnish

Sea salt and freshly ground black pepper

1 Heat the vegetable oil in a deep casserole and fry the venison in batches. Each piece should be carefully nurtured: you're aiming for a little caramelising on each bit of meat, as it will make your stew taste all the richer. Set the browned venison aside on a waiting plate while you crack on with the rest.

2 If necessary, add a little more oil to the pot and sauté the onions and garlic for about 5 minutes until they are beginning to caramelise.

3 Return your delicious venison to the pot and sprinkle over the flour. Give everything a good stir until the flour has all but disappeared. Throw in the carrots, swede, thyme and bay, pour over the red wine and beef stock and bring to a simmer. Reduce the heat and allow your pot to gently cook for 1¼ hours.

4 Remove the lid and stir through the chestnuts and cranberry sauce. Season and garnish with some fresh parsley before serving.

PIG POTS

Only those who know me very well will realise that this is a special chapter. As a little girl I would request that car journeys be diverted via pig farms so I could pin my face to the window and track the curly pink tails snuffling into their tin houses. My birthday presents were, on more than one occasion, pictures of the pink princesses or illustrated books teaching me the history of pigs and their importance in British arts. The *pièce de resistance*? Austin, the aged farmer who lived up the road, calling his two enormously spoilt Gloustershire Old Spots Georgina and Caroline, after my sister and me. Never, ever, have I felt so proud.

I don't remember discovering that this icon of mine was the source of sausages, lardons and bacon, but somehow the knowledge only added to my interest. Within this chapter is a delicious assortment of cuts that create very yummy dishes that will crown any table.

BAKED SAUSAGES
WITH SWEET POTATO & FENNEL

British bangers deserve the iconic status they have been given and I'm only sorry that many of us eat them accompanied by loose 'smash' or as blackened crusts from the BBQ. Here is a colourful and hearty autumnal dish. It's ideal for a midweek supper to show off our British heritage and give the sausage a bit of a makeover.

PREP TIME 15 MINUTES   SERVES 4   COOK TIME 45 MINUTES

500g sweet potatoes (approx. 2 large ones), peeled

1 healthy-sized fennel bulb

3 garlic cloves, peeled and sliced

1 teaspoon celery seeds

1 tablespoon dark brown sugar

3 tablespoons olive oil

8 solid, good-quality sausages

8 smoked back bacon rashers

1 tablespoon plain flour

100ml apple juice

50ml dry white wine

2 tablespoons balsamic vinegar

1 or 2 sprigs of thyme, or fennel fronds if you can find them

Sea salt and freshly ground black pepper

1 Preheat the oven to 200°C/gas mark 6. To start, roughly chop the sweet potato into good 4cm chunks and chop the fennel into 1cm slices across the bulb and then divide into the natural cresents. Place in a large roasting tin with the garlic, celery seeds and brown sugar. Drizzle over the olive oil and give everything a good muddle so all the vegetables are coated. Season well.

2 Wrap each sausage snugly in a rasher of bacon so it looks mummified and then nestle in with the vegetables. Roast the whole lot in the oven for 25 minutes.

3 Lightly sprinkle over the flour and jiggle the dish until it's disappeared and has been incorporated among the vegetables. Pour over the apple juice, white wine and balsamic vinegar, add the herbs, then continue to roast for a further 20 minutes until everything is cooked through, the sauce is thickened and the kitchen is smelling delicious. Serve with a glass of cold cider!

TREACLE BAKED BEANS

There are not many dishes I crave for breakfast, a simple lunch or indeed a Sunday supper, but this recipe ticks each of these very crucial boxes. It's as versatile as a fold-up bicycle on a city commute. I think the key to a wonderfully gloopy dish is laidback, gentle cooking and a generous helping of molasses or black treacle. Make an enormous pot and freeze tubs for those cold, blustery moments when you feel like a hug and there are no hugs to be found.

PREP TIME 20 MINUTES   **SERVES 6**   COOK TIME 7–9 HOURS

500g dried white beans or cannellini beans, rinsed

1 large onion, cut in half

2 fresh bay leaves

125ml maple syrup

100g dark brown sugar

1 tablespoon black treacle

½ tablespoon chilli flakes

1 teaspoon salt

1 tablespoon Worcesterhire sauce

1 tablespoon Dijon mustard

200g bacon lardons

1 First, prepare your beans. Put the beans, onion and bay leaves in a 2-litre pot and cover with 2.5 litres cold water. Simmer, uncovered, for about 1 hour or until the beans are tender. Drain the beans. Discard the onion and bay leaves.

2 To the now-empty pot add the maple syrup, brown sugar, treacle, chilli flakes, salt, Worcestershire sauce and Dijon mustard along with 600ml water. Bring to a simmer and cook, over a medium heat, for a few minutes until the sauce has come together.

3 Add the beans to the sauce along with the bacon lardons. Leave to cook on a very low heat for 6–8 hours, until the beans melt in your mouth like butter and the sauce has become deliciously syrupy. Stir as often as you feel like.

 TIP – THESE BEANS FREEZE BEAUTIFULLY SO DON'T BE SCARED OF MAKING A HUGE BATCH, DIVIDING INTO TUPPERWARE AND FREEZING FOR LATER IN THE MONTH.

PROSCIUTTO & CHIVE OMELETTE

PREP TIME 5 MINUTES • COOK TIME 6 MINUTES

Omelettes are the ultimate simple supper, especially when the cupboards are looking bare. Eggs, a pinch of salt and one or two other key ingredients are seemingly thrown together like a last-minute outfit but the results are exquisite (the culinary equivalent of a Bafta ball gown, I suppose).

SERVES 2

4 large free-range eggs, beaten
3–4 slices of prosciutto, torn into strips
2 tablespoons finely chopped chives
20g butter
Sea salt and freshly ground black pepper

1 Crack the eggs into a small mixing bowl and lightly beat with a fork. Drop the prosciutto and chives into the bowl and season, season, season.

2 Heat the butter in a medium-sized (approx. 20cm) frying pan until it begins to crackle and cover the base. Keep the heat high and pour in the egg mixture. With a spatula at the ready, draw the outside edges (which will cook more quickly) towards the gooey centre. Allow any liquid mixture to move into the gaps.

3 Continue with this action for about 2 minutes; don't forget that the omelette will continue to cook once the pan is removed from the heat.

4 Fold the omelette in half and divide between two plates, as neatly as you wish, and serve with a spot of salad.

PEA, PARMA HAM & MINT FRITTATA

PREP TIME 10 MINUTES • COOK TIME 15 MINUTES

The glorious frittata is perfect for summer picnics.

MAKES 6 BIG TRIANGLES

2 tablespoons olive oil
1 medium onion, roughly chopped
2 garlic cloves, peeled and finely chopped
½ teaspoon cayenne pepper
9 medium free-range eggs
150g frozen peas
80g Parmesan cheese, finely grated
3 tablespoons roughly chopped mint
6 slices of Parma ham, torn into strips
Sea salt and freshly ground black pepper

1 Put half the olive oil in a 23cm non-stick frying pan. Add the onion and fry until translucent, then add the garlic and cayenne and cook for 1 minute. Remove from the pan and cool slightly.

2 Crack the eggs into a large bowl and gently mix. Stir through the fried onion, frozen peas, three-quarters of the Parmesan and the mint. This is your opportunity to season radically, so crack that pepper. Stir well to combine. Preheat the grill to high.

3 Put the frying pan back on a low heat and add the remaining olive oil. Heat for about 30 seconds. Pour the egg mixture into the pan in a gorgeous heap and lie the Parma strips on the surface. Gently cook for about 10 minutes until the base is firm and the frittata is cooked 1–2cm from the edge but the centre is still a little wobbly. Sprinkle over the remaining Parmesan.

4 Transfer the pan to the grill and cook until the top is golden and puffed like a peacock. Don't overcook as the frittata will continue to cook in the residual heat. Remove and allow to cool for a few minutes before serving in wedges.

MANCHEGO, PANCETTA
& LEEK RISOTTO

Risotto is a blank canvas that is dressed according to your mood – this punchy combination of manchego and pancetta oozes sophistication and catapults a humble risotto into a meal worthy of royalty, or even just a very good friend.

PREP TIME 10 MINUTES	SERVES 2	COOK TIME 35 MINUTES

2 tablespoons olive oil

2 small leeks, chopped into 0.5cm rounds

100g smoked pancetta, diced

A knob of butter

200g Arborio or Carnaroli risotto rice

850ml hot chicken stock

2 tablespoons red pesto

50g Manchego cheese, grated

Sea salt and freshly ground black pepper

1 Heat 1 tablespoon of the olive oil in a deep sauté pan over a high heat. Add the leeks and pancetta to the pan and fry for 4–5 minutes, until the leeks are looking tender and the pancetta is cooked through. Remove from the pan and set aside.

2 Add the remaining olive oil and the knob of butter to the pan and reduce the heat to low. Over a gentle heat, add the risotto rice and stir so the grains are coated in oily butter. Gradually add all but 100ml of the hot stock, one ladleful at a time, stirring each until it's absorbed before you think of adding the next; this will take about 25 minutes, so go slowly. Season.

3 When the risotto is al dente and the whole thing is looking sloppy, stir through the pesto and return the leeks and bacon to the pan (reserving a few pieces for garnish). Warm the risotto through and add the remaining 100ml of hot chicken stock if you think it's needed. Remove from the heat, stir through the Manchego and serve with the reserved leeks and pancetta and a good twist of black pepper on the top.

 TIP – IF YOU MAKE YOUR RISOTTO IN ADVANCE, STOP COOKING THE RICE A FEW MINUTES BEFORE IT'S DONE AND ALLOW TO COOL. TO SERVE, HEAT A PAN WITH A FEW SPOONFULS OF STOCK IN THE BOTTOM AND, WHEN BUBBLING, SPOON IN THE RISOTTO. CONTINUE TO ADD HOT STOCK UNTIL THE RICE IS COOKED AND THE CONSISTENCY IS THAT OF THICK PORRIDGE.

SPINACH, SALAMI & FETA QUESADILLAS

PREP TIME 5 MINUTES • COOK TIME 8 MINUTES

A quesadilla, for those who need clarification, is the Mexican equivalent of a toasted cheese sarnie – and I would say it definitely has the edge over its British counterpart for three reasons. First, in order to make it you don't need a machine that gathers dust for the majority of the year. Second, the quesadilla has an endearing communal feel about it, one large round being sliced into equal triangles. Third, generally the fillings are more varied. It's my food of choice for watching some sport or, more likely, a good old period drama on television.

SERVES 4

2 large flour tortillas
50g baby spinach
5 or 6 slices of salami, each torn roughly into 3
50g feta cheese, crumbled
75g strong farmhouse Cheddar cheese, finely grated
Sea salt and freshly ground black pepper

1 Here it is – just the one step, but make sure all the ingredients are ready as you don't have long once the pan is hot! Heat up a frying pan large enough to hold a tortilla. Once it's hot, place the tortilla in the bottom of the pan (no oil needed) and sprinkle the ingredients on the top with a good grinding of black pepper. Sandwich with the other tortilla and cook until the bottom one starts to turn golden, about 4–5 minutes. Being careful, flip it over (I might use a large chopping board placed over the frying pan to help me do this). Cook the other side for a couple of minutes. Done in less than 10 minutes. Now turn on the telly and cut the quesadilla into quarters to serve.

PUMPKIN PARCELS WITH BACON & SAGE

PREP TIME 10 MINUTES • COOK TIME 1–1¼ HOURS

For a few weeks every year shelves are inundated with pumpkins awaiting their callous fate of becoming contorted expressions. If you do resist the urge to grab a scalpel and opt to cook your pumpkin instead, here is a super-simple suggestion. The baked crescents could be eaten for lunch just so or served with some grilled sausages for an easy dinner.

SERVES 6

1kg pumpkin, deseeded and cut into 4–5 wedges
   (leave the skin on)
12–14 streaky bacon rashers
12 sage leaves
2 tablespoons extra virgin olive oil
Sea salt and freshly ground black pepper
A drizzle of maple syrup and lamb's lettuce, to serve

1 Preheat the oven to 170°C/gas mark 3.

2 Wrap each pumpkin wedge in 3 or 4 rashers of bacon and weave the sage leaves amongst the bacon.

3 Lie the wrapped edges on a lightly oiled baking tray and then drizzle with the olive oil. Season and bake in the oven for 1–1¼ hours until the pumpkin is tender. Serve drizzled with maple syrup aboard a pile of lamb's lettuce.

HAM, MUSTARD
& PARSLEY TARTIFLETTE

There is a logical association linking tartiflette to cold French mountains – not many recipes can deliver such a concentration of calories that keeps skiers flying down the slopes until dusk. I would argue that a harsh frost anywhere in the world renders us all in need of a good tartiflette. This one has salty ham and Camembert hidden within the potato layers and is ideal for stomachs that require energy loading. A healthy green salad is all that is needed to accompany it.

PREP TIME 20 MINUTES   SERVES 6   COOK TIME 2 HOUR

A little oil, for greasing

1kg waxy potatoes, peeled

1 large onion, peeled

Approx. 3 thick slices of ham (200g), torn

1 whole 250g Camembert cheese, torn into 2cm chunks

3 tablespoons roughly chopped flat-leaf parsley,
    plus 1 tablespoon to serve

1 tablespoon Dijon mustard

200ml hot vegetable stock

300ml double cream (not single as it will split
    during cooking)

Sea salt and freshly ground black pepper

1 Preheat the oven to 180°C/gas mark 4. Brush the inside of a generous 2-litre ovenproof dish with olive oil.

2 Your first job is to do the slicing – after that it's a doddle. Start with the potatoes, which need to be about 4–5mm thick; you will need a steady hand and a sharp knife or a food processor. Next are the onions, again 5mm.

3 Now it's as easy as a dot-to-dot. Start by placing roughly a fifth of the potato slices on the bottom of the ovenproof dish. Season and then layer with roughly a quarter of the ham, onion rings, torn Camembert and parsley. Top with another fifth of potato slices and, using your hands, apply a bit of pressure to compress the layer. Continue with the other layers until all the ingredients have been used up. By my estimation there will be four layers, and then a final layer of potato slices.

4 Dot the top with mustard and gently pour over the hot stock and then the cream. Season again. Cover with greased foil (this is important or the foil will stick to the potatoes) and bake in the oven for 1 hour. Remove the foil and sprinkle over the remaining parsley. Bake, uncovered, for 1 more hour.

5 Remove the dish from the oven and allow it to sit in a warm place for 20–30 minutes before serving. It will still be perfectly hot but everything will have 'come to'.

HAM HOCK

BUTTER BEAN & PARSLEY BROTH

You could be forgiven for feeling some confusion at the butcher's counter as pork shanks, ham hocks and pig knuckles are all the same cut; in other words, you can use any of them. The masses haven't quite cottoned on to this joint, so it's still wonderfully cheap to buy and two or three hocks can feed an army.

PREP TIME 20 MINUTES · SERVES 6–8 · COOK TIME 4 HOURS

2 ham hocks (each weighing 1–1.5kg)
1 large onion, roughly chopped
3 plump garlic cloves, peeled and sliced
3 sticks of celery, cut into 3cm chunks

3 large carrots, peeled and cut into 3cm chunks
1 bunch of flat-leaf parsley, stalks chopped and
   green leaves kept for garnishing
2 x 400g tins butter beans, drained

1 Put the ham hocks into a 5-litre saucepan and cover with cold water. Bring to the boil and allow to bubble for 10 minutes. Drain away the scummy water and refill the pot with 3 litres of cold water.

2 Bring the fresh water to the boil and gently simmer, uncovered, for 2½ hours, skimming the residue occasionally until the ham is cooked and the meat is falling off the bone. Add the onion, garlic, celery, carrots and parsley stalks to the pot and stir through the beautiful ham stock. Remove the lid and cook for 1 more hour.

3 Remove the ham hocks from the pot using an enormous spoon or tongs and, once they are cool enough to handle, pick out the big chunks of meat and discard the fat and bones; the meat should fall easily off the bone. Don't be alarmed by the surprising amount of fat on these knuckles. Using your fingers, tear the ham into bite-sized shreds.

4 Return the shredded ham to the pot and add the butter beans. Simmer for 5–10 minutes to allow the beans to break down slightly, then remove from the heat. The consistency should be gloopy and that of a thick broth, so continue to boil if the stock needs to reduce further.

5 Just before serving, garnish with the parsley leaves and season as required. My vote would be to serve this in warmed shallow bowls with some fluffy warm bread.

 TIP – DON'T BE SURPRISED IF YOU RETURN TO ANY LEFTOVERS THE FOLLOWING DAY AND FIND THE GELATINE HAS SET THE BROTH SOLID. SIMPLY REHEAT OVER A LOW HEAT AND YOU'RE BACK IN BUSINESS FOR SECONDS.

PORK & PISTACHIO MEATLOAF

PREP TIME 20 MINUTES • COOK TIME 35 MINUTES

A cluster of recipes have been tarnished by associations with wartime, and sadly meatloaf is one of them. But this dish is due for a makeover and needs to be firmly pinned back on the culinary map. Let's look at the positives: it can be eaten hot or cold, summer or winter, it's super-quick to do, cheap as chips to make and wonderfully nutritious to eat. I've stuffed flavour into this recipe and it's begging to be given a shot.

MAKES 10 SLICES

100g white breadcrumbs

150g pistachio nuts, roughly chopped

1kg minced pork

50g pickled gherkins, chopped into pieces

1 tablespoon English mustard

3 garlic cloves, peeled and crushed

2 medium free-range eggs, beaten

Sea salt and freshly ground black pepper

Fresh thyme, to serve

1 Preheat the oven to 180°C/gas mark 4. Line the base of a 900g non-stick loaf tin with greaseproof paper.

2 Combine all of the ingredients in one enormous bowl. Get your hands involved to really squidge everything together. Season, season, season.

3 Pack down the mixture into the loaf tin as best you can and bake in the oven for 35 minutes, until the loaf is firm to the touch. Allow it to 'come to' for about 10 minutes before turning it out. Leave to cool, then slice and serve with the pickled cucumber (see right) and a sprig of fresh thyme.

PICKLED CUCUMBER

PREP TIME 10 MINUTES (PLUS 1 HOUR COOLING)
• COOK TIME 10 MINUTES

Try this lip-smacking pickle with your meatloaf.

MAKES 1 x 250ML JAR

60ml white wine vinegar

Juice of 1 lime

1 tablespoon black mustard seeds

40g caster sugar

½ tablespoon salt

½ medium cucumber, cut into 4mm slices on the angle

100g radishes, topped, tailed and large ones cut in half

A small clump of fennel fronds or 1 tablespoon chopped dill

1 Simply pour the vinegar, lime juice, mustard seeds, salt and sugar into a small saucepan. Bring to simmering point and stir for a minute or so, until the sugar dissolves. Allow to cool.

2 Squeeze the cucumber, radishes and fennel fronds (or dill) into your waiting, sterilised jar and pour over the pickling liquid. Seal tightly and wait for at least 4 hours before tucking in.

ROSE HARISSA PORK
WITH QUINOA & DATES

Eeeshhh… there's a fine line between cooking pork fillet too much (when the meat will be as dry as a bone) or too little, when it'll be too pink – and too pink pork isn't good for anybody. I've cooked this recipe, in which the pork fillet is covered and nestled among quinoa, stock and juicy dates, so there should be no danger of tough meat. It's a beautiful recipe, a slightly different take on a tagine. My husband said it was 'damn good', which I think is a thumbs up.

PREP TIME 10 MINUTES   SERVES 2–3   COOK TIME 35 MINUTES

1 tablespoon olive oil
300–400g pork tenderloin
1 medium onion, roughly chopped
1½ tablespoons rose harissa paste
100g quinoa

80g dried dates, pitted and roughly chopped
3 large, ripe tomatoes, roughly chopped
400ml hot chicken stock
4 tablespoons roughly chopped flat-leaf parsley
Sea salt and freshly ground black pepper

1 Preheat the oven to 180°C/gas mark 4.

2 Heat the oil in the base of a shallow, ovenproof pot over a high heat. Season your meat and, using tongs, sear the pork on all sides until beautifully golden. Remove from the pot and set aside to rest.

3 Add a drop more oil to the pot if needed and fry the onion for a few minutes until translucent, then stir through the harissa. Add the quinoa, dates, tomatoes and just 300ml of the hot stock. Give everything a good muddle, season well and simmer for 10 minutes. Stir through the remaining stock and half the parsley once the 10 minutes are up.

4 Place the pork fillet on top of your quinoa mixture and place the pot in the oven for 20 minutes, covered, until the quinoa is plump and the pork is cooked through. Remove from the oven and allow the dish to sit for 5–7 minutes so the pork can rest and 'come to'.

5 Sprinkle generously with the rest of the parsley, and serve the pork sliced on a bed of quinoa.

MELTING POT BELLY
WITH FENNEL & ROSEMARY

When cooked correctly, pork belly has a blistered skin that cracks, brittle like an icy puddle, fat that renders to a glorious slush and meat that pulls apart with the slightest nudge. This dish isn't difficult so should help you to achieve just that – I have a wonderful friend who unashamedly stole this recipe and cooked it four times in as many dinner parties, achieving perfection each and every time.

PREP TIME 10 MINUTES   SERVES 4–6   COOK TIME 3½ HOURS

1.5kg boneless pork belly

1 tablespoon sea salt

1 tablespoon finely chopped rosemary

1 tablespoon olive oil

1 red onion, cut into quarters

10–12 garlic cloves, peeled and cut in half

2 fennel bulbs, cut into 3cm wedges

3 sticks of celery, cut into large chunks

500ml hot chicken stock

Freshly ground black pepper

Crème fraîche, to serve

1 Preheat the oven to 220°C/gas mark 7. Using a sharp knife, score the skin of your pork belly in diagonal lines approximately 2.5cm apart, taking care only to score the fat and not cut into the meat. Rub the sea salt and rosemary deep into the fat and season with black pepper. Drizzle with olive oil.

2 Place the belly in a roasting dish that's big enough for the meat to lie flat and roast in the oven for about 30 minutes. You will see the skin start to become crispy crackling. After 30 minutes, turn the heat down to 180°C/gas mark 4 and roast for 1 hour more.

3 Remove the meat from the oven and carefully place it on a board. Reduce the oven temperature to 170°C/gas mark 3. Tip all the vegetables into the roasting dish and smother with the fat. Pour the stock into the roasting dish. Return the belly back to the top of the vegetables and roast in the oven for a further 1½–2 hours. The pork is ready to serve when it almost falls away to the touch.

4 Once it's wonderfully tender, remove the pork from the dish and cut into chunks with a sharp knife. Serve with the braised vegetables and a dollop of crème fraîche.

CARAMELISED PORK

CHORIZO & BLACK PUDDING STEW (FABADA ASTURIANA)

My first taste of *fabada asturiana* was sitting in a rustic Spanish restaurant. Formica tables and red plastic bread baskets coloured the room in which a round woman ladled the only menu choice into shallow bowls, spilling precious stock as she went. I asked for the recipe and here it is, with one or two tweaks that may have been lost in translation.

PREP TIME 30 MINUTES
(PLUS OVERNIGHT SOAKING)

SERVES 8

COOK TIME 3 HOURS

500g dried white beans

400g pork shoulder, cut into 3–4cm chunks

200g cooking chorizo

1 x 150g black pudding

6–8 smoked bacon rashers

1 onion, finely sliced

2 carrots, peeled and chopped

A few strands of saffron

Sprigs of flat-leaf parsley, to garnish

1 Now, you'll have to think ahead a little for this one and get going the evening before your dish is needed. Soak the white beans overnight in a bowl of cold water and soak the pork in another.

2 When you are ready to begin, drain the beans and tip into a 4–5-litre pot. Cover with fresh cold water. Bring to the boil and simmer over a gentle heat for about an hour, skimming off any residue that makes its way to the surface.

3 Add the drained pork, chorizo, black pudding, bacon, onion, carrots and saffron. Add a little more cold water, making sure all the ingredients are just submerged, and bring back to a simmer. Cook for 2 hours, or until the meat and beans are perfectly tender. Stir occasionally to make sure the bottom isn't catching.

4 Remove the pot from the heat and fish out the black pudding, chorizo and bacon. Once they have cooled a little, slice each up into small chunks and set aside. (In Spain, this mixture is traditionally known as the *compango*).

5 Ladle some beans and liquid into your serving bowls and top with a selection of the *compango*. Sprinkle with oodles of parsley and serve.

PIGS' CHEEKS
WITH CARROTS & CIDER

My very patient husband has eaten with me throughout writing this book and if he were to pick his favourite dish this would win gold. Pigs' cheeks, which are exquisite pillows of tender pork about the size of a halved plum, should be cooked when you aren't in a rush and have time to enjoy the preparation. It is obvious that they sit sublimely well alongside a good glug of cider and some scented thyme.

PREP TIME 25 MINUTES   **SERVES 4**   COOK TIME 2¾ HOURS

2 tablespoons vegetable oil

1kg pigs' cheeks

150g pancetta lardons

2 onions, finely sliced

1 teaspoon ground ginger

3 carrots, peeled and cut into bite-sized chunks

½ large celeriac, peeled and chopped into bite-sized chunks

2 garlic cloves, peeled and sliced

2 tablespoons plain flour

A bundle of thyme, tied together with kitchen string

440ml cider

300ml vegetable stock

50ml double cream

1 tablespoon wholegrain mustard

Sea salt and freshly ground black pepper

Pea shoots or flat-leaf parsley, chopped, to garnish

1 Heat the oil in a large heavy-based pan and, over a high heat, fry the pigs' cheeks, 4 or 5 at a time, until browned on both sides. Remove from the pan and set aside. Fry the pancetta until crispy and set aside with the cheeks.

2 Lower the heat and gently sauté the onions with the ground ginger until soft; you may need to add a touch more oil. Add the carrots, celeriac and garlic and cook for a few minutes until they begin to soften. Return the pigs' cheeks and lardons to the pot and sprinkle over the flour. Stir to coat until you can no longer see the flour.

3 Throw in the bundle of thyme, the cider and vegetable stock. Season and bring to a simmer, then reduce the heat, cover and cook for 2½ hours. Remove the lid for the last 30 minutes.

4 With a large slotted spoon, remove all 'the bits' so you can finish off the sauce. Pour in the cream and mustard. Bring the liquid to the boil and bubble for about 10 minutes until the sauce has thickened. Return all the meat to the pot and serve garnished with a pile of pea shoots or freshly chopped parsley.

FOUR HOOVES: BEEF & LAMB

The old proverb, 'God sends meat and the devil sends cooks', seems particularly apt when we're faced with a fillet steak or loin of lamb. Pressure is on from the moment the quite large wad of cash is handed over and really it's only the chef to be blamed if something goes wrong. Stewing meat, on the other hand, marbled with fat and stacked with flavour, is certainly more forgiving and relies a little more on the ingredients it mingles with. Initially there is slightly more work, but once you've done the chopping, making a slow-cooked pot requires less effort than going as yourself to a fancy dress party.

Hidden among these recipes are cuts that you will almost certainly be familiar with, but I hope I can also encourage you to try the odd shin of beef or shank of lamb. They create wonderful centrepieces that will make any recipient love you just a little bit more.

BURGUNDY BEEF
WITH STILTON DUMPLINGS

Of course you can make this recipe with another red wine, perhaps Merlot or Malbec, but I believe the richer the wine, the more delicious the end result. Paired with the Stilton dumplings and a dash of brandy, this is a gentleman's club embodied in an honoured stew. All that's needed is a post-dinner cigar and a smoking jacket.

PREP TIME 30 MINUTES   SERVES 6   COOK TIME 2½ HOURS

2 tablespoons olive oil

1kg shin of beef, trimmed of fat and cut into 3cm cubes

2 onions, roughly chopped

2 tablespoons plain flour, seasoned

4 garlic cloves, peeled and cut in half

4 carrots, scrubbed and cut into 3cm lengths

4 small parsnips, scrubbed, chopped lengthways
    and then into chunks

3–4 sprigs of thyme

500ml Burgundy

2 tablespoons brandy

500ml beef stock

FOR THE DUMPLINGS

125g self-raising flour

50g butter, softened

40g Stilton cheese, crumbled

1 tablespoon roughly chopped flat-leaf parsley

3–4 tablespoons cold water

1 Heat the oil in the bottom of a deep casserole over a high heat. Sear the beef in batches until each piece has begun to caramelise, and set aside. Add the onions to the casserole, reduce the heat slightly and fry until soft. Return the meat to the pot, sprinkle with the flour and stir to combine.

2 Add the garlic, carrots, parsnips, thyme, wine, brandy and beef stock to the pot (i.e everything else). Bring to simmering point, reduce the heat, then cover and simmer for 2½ hours. Every so often give your stew a good stir to stop it sticking to the bottom of the pan. And don't be afraid to add a little water if you think it's looking dry as every hob cooks at a slightly different temperature.

3 Meanwhile, make the dumplings. Rub the butter into the flour and mix with the Stilton and parsley. Add enough cold water to bring the mixture together to a soft dough and divide into 5–6 dumplings.

4 Fifteen minutes before the end of the stew's cooking time, drop the dumplings onto its surface and continue to cook, covered, for the final 15 minutes, until the clouds puff and you have edible blotting paper. Serve.

SOY CHILLI BEEF

This Asian-inspired casserole uses lean steak which, though a little more expensive, makes for a super speedy supper option. If you suddenly have six hungry mouths to feed, don't be afraid to make it stretch with a little more sweet potato. Serve with steamed rice.

PREP TIME 15 MINUTES · SERVES 4 · COOK TIME 25 MINUTES

2 tablespoons vegetable oil

2 onions, roughly chopped

3 garlic cloves, peeled and finely chopped

2 tablespoons plain flour

1 teaspoon five spice

2–3 star anise

3 red peppers, deseeded and cut into chunky strips

1 large or 2 medium sweet potatoes (about 500g cubed weight), peeled and cut into 3cm chunks

2 fresh red chillies, deseeded and finely chopped, or 2 teaspoons dried chilli flakes

2 tablespoons dark brown sugar

3 tablespoons dark soy sauce

600ml hot beef stock

600g beef rump steaks, cut into thin, bite-sized strips (best sliced across the grain)

A small handful of coriander sprigs, to garnish

Freshly ground black pepper

1 Heat the vegetable oil in a heavy-bottomed casserole over a high heat. Add the onion, reduce the heat to medium and soften for approximately 5 minutes, adding in the garlic for the last minute.

2 Stir through the flour, then throw in the five spice, star anise, peppers, sweet potatoes and chopped (or flaked) chillies. Sprinkle with the brown sugar, season with black pepper and heat through for a minute or so.

3 Add the soy sauce and beef stock and bring to the boil. Reduce the heat, cover and simmer for 15 minutes or until the sweet potatoes are tender. Add the beef strips to the pot for the final 5 minutes of this time. Cover and simmer until they just cook in the broth and are beautifully tender.

4 Serve each portion topped with a pert sprig of coriander.

 TIP – TRY USING TENDER CHICKEN INSTEAD OF THE BEEF AND REMOVING THE CHILLIES TO MAKE THIS BROTH SUITABLE FOR LITTLE PEOPLE.

BEEF, PRUNE
& ROSEMARY CASSEROLE

Like French cheese and wildflower meadows, some stews (most, in fact) mature with age. After a day or two in the fridge, richer and sweeter notes come dancing through. With this recipe in particular the delicate sugars of the prunes take hold and the steak becomes ever more tender, so think ahead, fellow cooks, and start preparing.

PREP TIME 20 MINUTES · SERVES 6 · COOK TIME 2½ HOURS

3 tablespoons vegetable oil

250g pancetta, cut into 1cm cubes

750g chuck steak or stewing beef, diced

400g shallots, peeled but kept whole

300g chestnut mushrooms, thickly sliced

4 garlic cloves, peeled and each cut into 3

250g prunes, halved and stoned

2 tablespoons plain flour

75ml sherry vinegar

800ml hot beef stock

4–5 sprigs of rosemary, plus extra for sprinkling

700g Maris Piper potatoes, sliced into thin
    (2–3mm) rounds

Sea salt and freshly ground black pepper

1 Preheat the oven to 190°C/gas mark 5.

2 Heat 1 tablespoon of the oil in the bottom of a casserole. Start with the pancetta and fry until it's crispy and smells like Sunday mornings. Set aside and continue with the beef. Fry this in two or three batches so the pan doesn't overcrowd, and keep the heat up so the meat browns, adding more oil when needed. This will take a few minutes, but don't be tempted to miss out this step and 'make do' with only grey meat. You'll taste the colour. Remove the beef from the casserole and set aside with the pancetta.

3 Next up are the shallots. Fry until the edges begin to brown. Remove and add to the waiting meat. Finally, fry

the mushrooms over a high heat until crispy, adding in the garlic for the last minute or so.

4 Return the beef, pancetta and shallots to the pan and add the prunes. Stir through the flour and season well. Pour over the sherry vinegar and allow it to bubble off before adding the stock and rosemary sprigs. Cook, covered, in the oven for 1 hour.

5 Arrange your potato slices on the surface of the stew like the apples on a French apple tart. Season again, sprinkle with chopped rosemary and return to the oven for 30 minutes. Remove the lid and cook for a final 30 minutes or until the potatoes are tender. Serve piping hot.

TIP – IF YOU ARE IN A HURRY, PARBOIL YOUR SLICED POTATOES AND ADD THEM TO THE TOP OF THE CASSEROLE – THEY SHOULD ONLY TAKE 20 MINUTES TO COOK THROUGH.

POT-ROAST BRISKET
WITH PORCINI & BARLEY

Here is a really impressive one pot with oodles of flavour and a variety of ingredients that may push you to step out of your comfort zone. The barley loves being cooked for so long and results in hundreds of plump cushions supporting the tender beef.

PREP TIME 20 MINUTES | **SERVES 6** | COOK TIME 3½ HOURS

30g dried porcini mushrooms
2–3 tablespoons olive oil
1.5–1.8kg rolled beef brisket
2 medium onions, roughly chopped
3 garlic cloves, peeled and sliced
½ teaspoon dried chilli flakes

200g pearl barley
30g butter
3 sprigs of rosemary
1.2 litres hot beef stock
Sea salt and freshly ground black pepper

1 Soak the porcini in 500ml boiling water for 30 minutes. Remove the mushrooms, reserving the precious liquid, and squeeze dry in your hands. Finely chop and set aside.

2 Preheat the oven to 170°C/gas mark 3.

3 Place a deep, 5-litre, ovenproof casserole over a high heat. Add the olive oil and, using tongs to steady the meat, brown the beef all over. Remove and set aside to a waiting plate. Reduce the heat slightly and add the chopped onions, garlic and chilli flakes. Cook for 4–5 minutes until the onion has softened and you can smell the garlic. Season with salt and freshly ground black pepper.

4 Stir through the pearl barley and butter. Add the chopped porcini to the pot with their cooking liquid and throw in the rosemary. Nestle the browned beef in the centre of the pot and pour the hot beef stock around, taking care not to pour on top of the meat. Stir gently to make sure all the ingredients are perfectly combined and cover with a tight-fitting lid. Cook in the oven for 3 hours, stirring once or twice to ensure nothing is catching on the bottom of the pot.

5 When you finally remove the pot from the oven and unveil the roast, stir through a little boiling water to loosen the barley, if you think it's necessary. I would suggest removing the beef from the pot in order to slice it, before plating up with a good spoonful of the barley.

BEEF, LENTIL
& GREEN OLIVE STEW

I've given this stew a little personality. The base is one you'll be familiar with, but note the addition of lentils, ground cloves and olives. Lentils will enrich the sauce while the olives do the seasoning for you with an Italian salty bite to enhance a thoroughly British classic. Make it in advance if you know you are in for a busy weekend. This dish doesn't mind being kept waiting.

PREP TIME 40 MINUTES · · · · · · · · **PLENTY FOR 8** · · · · · · · · COOK TIME 2½ HOURS

2 tablespoons olive oil

1.5kg stewing steak, trimmed of fat and cut into
   3–4cm pieces

400g shallots

3 tablespooons seasoned flour

½ teaspoon cayenne pepper

¼ teaspoon ground cloves

300ml medium-bodied red wine

3 sticks of celery, chopped into 3cm pieces

3 fresh bay leaves

2 garlic cloves, peeled but kept whole

500ml hot beef stock

800g tomatoes, chopped

200g Puy lentils

150g fat green olives

Sea salt

Freshly chopped flat-leaf parsley, to serve

Sour cream, to serve

1 Heat the oil in the bottom of a large casserole. Fry the beef in batches until golden brown all over, adding an extra glug of oil with every new batch if you feel it needs it. Remove the meat from the pot and set aside.

2 Meanwhile, put the shallots in a large bowl. Cover with boiling water and leave for a few minutes, then drain and cool down by placing in cold water. Peel, trim the bases and cut any large shallots in half. Add to the casserole and fry until just beginning to caramelise, about 3–4 minutes.

3 Return the fried steak to the pan and sprinkle over the flour, cayenne pepper and ground cloves. Stir until the flour and spices are all incorporated. Add the red wine and bring to the boil, allowing it to bubble for a minute or so until the alcohol has evaporated. Reduce the heat to low and add the celery, bay leaves, garlic, beef stock, chopped tomatoes and lentils to the pot. Give your stew a little pinch of salt – you won't need any pepper because the cayenne ticks that box.

4 Cover with a tight-fitted lid and simmer, on a low heat, for 1½ hours, stirring occasionally to make sure the bottom of the stew isn't catching. Remove the lid and add the olives 30 minutes before the end of cooking.

5 Serve with a dollop of sour cream and chopped parsley.

WARMING BEEF SHIN
WITH CRUNCHY MUSTARD CROÛTONS

Beef shin has fabulous strips of collagen keeping all the muscles together, which melt to form a sticky stew, so don't be alarmed when you first glance at the meat (some would say fat equals flavour!). You could make the stew in advance and just add the croûtons on the night to make this an easy yet thoroughly entertaining recipe. Serve with a good pile of mash for a seriously hearty supper.

PREP TIME 30 MINUTES | SERVES 6 | COOK TIME 3½ HOURS

1.5kg piece of beef shin, cut into 4–5cm pieces

4 tablespoons vegetable oil

3 large onions, thickly sliced

4–5 garlic cloves, peeled and sliced

2 tablespoons plain flour

75ml balsamic vinegar

500ml brown ale

1 fresh bouquet garni (1 sprig fresh thyme, 1 fresh bay leaf and 2–3 parsley stalks, tied with kitchen string)

Sea salt and freshly ground black pepper

FOR THE CROÛTONS

2 tablespoons softened butter

2 tablespoons Dijon mustard

1 tablespoon fresh thyme leaves

1 x 300g ciabatta loaf, cut into 8–10 slices

1 Remove any unwanted sinew or large bits of fat from the meat, but don't be too perfect about this – you want some fat remaining to enhance the flavour of the stew. Blot the meat on kitchen paper; this will help prevent it sticking to the bottom of the saucepan.

2 Preheat the oven to 180°C/gas mark 4. Heat a good glug of oil in a large, ovenproof casserole. Add the meat in batches and seal the edges over a high heat. Don't rush this step; it will make the stew taste all the richer. As each piece is done, remove and set aside, adding a little more oil to the pot if needed.

3 Add more oil and fry the onions and garlic for 3–4 minutes until they are tinged with gold and have softened.

Return the beef shin to the pan. Sprinkle over the flour and stir until it's disappeared. Pour in the balsamic vinegar followed by the ale. Top up with water so the liquid is just covering the meat and add the bouquet garni. Season. Cover with a tight-fitting lid and pop into the oven for 2½–3 hours. Check the dish every hour or so to make sure it isn't drying out – top up with a little water if necessary.

4 Meanwhile, make the croûtons. Combine the softened butter with the mustard and thyme and generously slather over the slices of bread. When the shin has done its time, remove the lid and pop the mustard croûtons on the surface, butter-side up. Return to the oven, covered, for a further 20 minutes. Serve and enjoy.

SLOW-COOKED VEAL
& RED WINE STEW

When winter sets in and cold air covers the country like a carpet, I crave warming stews. Here, slabs of veal shank are cooked by a similar method to the well-known one-pot, osso bucco. Literally translated, 'osso bucco' means 'bone with a hole', which refers to the piece of bone encasing an ample amount of rich marrow in its centre. During the lengthy cooking, the marrow melts into the sauce, leaving an open hole – thus the name (and an exceptionally tasty sauce). It is possible to source humanely reared veal – look out for British rose veal – so you can indulge in this stew with a clear conscience. Enjoy piled on a mound of buttery mash.

PREP TIME 40 MINUTES   SERVES 4   COOK TIME 2 HOURS

3 tablespoons extra-virgin olive oil

4 x 200–300g veal shanks, bone in

3 medium onions, each cut into 8 wedges

8 garlic cloves, peeled and thickly sliced

1½ teaspoons ground cinnamon

2 tablespoons plain flour

2 tablespoons tomato purée

300ml medium-bodied red wine

200ml beef stock

400g tomatoes, chopped

3 sprigs of rosemary

1 x 400g tin kidney beans, drained and rinsed

Sea salt and freshly ground black pepper

Fresh flat-leaf parsley, to garnish

Mashed potato, to serve

1 Heat 2 tablespoons of the oil in a large, heavy-based pot over a medium heat. Fry each of the veal shanks until they start to caramelise, about 4 minutes on each side. Remove them from the pot and set aside.

2 Add the remaining oil to the pot and fry the onions over a gentle heat until soft. Be careful not to let them catch – the burnt taste will come through in the final dish. Add the garlic and cinnamon to the pot and cook, over a lower heat, for a further minute.

3 Return the veal to the pot and sprinkle over the flour. Stir through the tomato purée and combine until the

flour has all but disappeared. Pour over the wine and turn up the heat, allowing the wine to bubble so the alcohol disappears.

4 Return the heat to low and add the beef stock, chopped tomatoes and rosemary. Season vigorously before covering and cooking for 2 hours or until the veal is perfectly tender and the marrow has melted into the sauce.

5 Stir in the kidney beans and warm through for a few minutes before serving dressed with fresh parsley, atop a heap of creamy mashed potato.

BONED LAMB SHOULDER

WITH WALNUT & MINT PESTO

As a child I disliked pesto, but as an adult I put away my childish ways. Pesto is now an absolute staple in my kitchen. A riot of flavours, it can be used to spice up any dressing, sandwich or, in this case, a heavenly hunk of lamb. If you are a dab hand with a butcher's knife, you can bone your own shoulder, but a quicker choice might be to ask the butcher kindly and watch in admiration as he delicately dances around the lamb, leaving you with not a bone in sight.

PREP TIME 20 MINUTES · SERVES 6 · COOK TIME – APPROX. 1 HOUR 40 MINUTES

1.7kg boned shoulder of lamb (weight of meat without shoulder bone)
1 small red onion, thinly sliced
2 tablespoons olive oil
600g carrots, scrubbed and cut into 3cm slices
600g potatoes, scrubbed and large ones cut in half
Sea salt and freshly ground black pepper

FOR THE PESTO
A bunch of mint (approx. 30g)
½ bunch flat-leaf parsley (approx. 10g)
3 garlic cloves, peeled
60g walnut halves
65ml extra virgin olive oil
½ teaspoon sea salt flakes

1 First, make the pesto. This is easy. Simply blend everything in a food processor, drizzling the oil in as you whiz. You want the pesto to be quite stiff, so refrain from adding any extra oil.

2 Preheat the oven to 220°C/gas mark 7. Spread the lamb wide open on a board, then slather it with the pesto and sprinkle over the red onion. Season well.

3 Using a long piece of kitchen string (I've used cotton in the absence of string before), tie the shoulder up into a watermelon shape. Season the outside and drizzle with olive oil – don't go overboard as the lamb will leech oil as it roasts. Calculate the cooking time at 20 minutes per 450g plus 20 minutes.

4 Roast in the oven for 20 minutes before dropping the temperature down to 190°C/gas mark 5 for the remainder of the cooking time.

5 Forty minutes before the end of the cooking time, nestle the carrots and potatoes into the pan. Coat in any oil that has escaped from the lamb.

6 When the lamb's ready, remove the string and place the meat onto a warmed serving dish. Leave to rest for 15 minutes before serving.

LAMB SHANKS
WITH ANCHOVY & FETA

The lamb shank is a cut that appeals for many reasons: first, each bone supports a hunk of flavourful meat, plenty to satisfy any appetite; second, enough fat is hidden among the tendons to produce a gloriously rich sauce; third, it doesn't cost a fortune; and lastly, even the most nervous of cooks couldn't muddle this up – your dinner will taste delicious.

PREP TIME 30 MINUTES   SERVES 4–6   COOK TIME 3½ HOURS

2 tablespoons olive oil

4 x lamb shanks (approx. 400g each)

2 onions, roughly chopped

1 tablespoon tomato purée

2 teaspoons sumac

40g tinned anchovies, drained and roughly chopped

1 whole head of garlic, outer papery leaves removed and the bulb cut in half horizontally

800g potatoes, scrubbed clean and cut into 4cm chunks

20g fresh oregano, tied into a bundle with kitchen string, plus extra to serve

450ml hot lamb stock

250ml red wine

Freshly ground black pepper

100g feta cheese, crumbled, to serve

1 Preheat the oven to 170°C/gas mark 3.

2 Heat the olive oil in a 6-litre, ovenproof casserole, then brown 2 shanks at a time, turning each shank regularly until the meat is evenly golden brown. Spend a good 10 minutes doing this; it is a good investment into your dish. Remove the shanks and set aside.

3 Add the onions to the pan and fry for 3–4 minutes until lightly golden. Stir through the tomato purée and sumac and heat through for a minute.

4 Add the chopped anchovies and head of garlic, and heat through for a minute or so before adding the potatoes and oregano bundle. Return the lamb shanks to the pot and pour over the lamb stock and red wine. Season with black pepper only – there will be enough salt coming from the anchovies.

5 Cover with a lid and cook in the oven, undisturbed, for 2½–3 hours until the lamb is trying to escape from the bone and the liquid has reduced. Remove the lid for the final 30 minutes of cooking if you think the sauce could be a little thicker.

6 Remove from the oven and allow to cool slightly before sprinkling over the feta and fresh oregano. Serve with tzatziki, if you like – homemade is best!

FOUR-HOUR
LAMB SHOULDER

Tender lamb falling apart with a gentle nudge from the back of a spoon must be any carnivore's fantasy (certainly mine). Serve with something fresh to lighten the plate – crème fraîche and some well-seasoned greens for example. Just a thought… you can also run a marathon in four hours. Both activites might require an afternoon nap and a healthy glass of red wine afterwards!

PREP TIME 20 MINUTES   SERVES 6   COOK TIME 4 HOURS

1 shoulder of lamb (approx. 2kg), bone in, trimmed
   of excess fat

3 or 4 rosemary sprigs

2 heads of garlic, cloves peeled and papery skin removed

2 red onions, each cut into 6 crescents

2 large carrots, peeled and sliced into 2.5cm rounds

2 turnips, peeled and cut into chunks

2 x 400g tins chopped tomatoes

2 fresh bay leaves

500ml red wine

Sea salt and freshly ground black pepper

1 Preheat the oven to 170°C/gas mark 3.

2 Prepare your lamb by making 10–15 incisions all over the top of the joint. Poke peeled garlic cloves and sprigs of rosemary into the holes and season well all over.

3 Place the onions, carrots and turnips in the bottom of the roasting tray and nestle the lamb on top. Add the chopped tomatoes, bay leaves and red wine to the tin. Season again.

4 Cover with a sheet of baking parchment, and then foil, and place in the preheated oven. Cook for 2 hours.

5 Reduce the heat to 150°C/gas mark 2. Remove the foil and parchment from the lamb, baste the meat and return to the oven to cook for a further 2 hours (check after 1½ hours in case you have a ferocious oven). The lamb will be ready when the meat is falling away from the bone. Skim off the fat and serve directly from the roasting tray.

LAMB STEW
WITH ARTICHOKES & SQUASHED TOMATOES

Slow cooking often takes me by surprise. After a few hours of close confinement, seemingly individual ingredients grow fond of one another and unite in a flavour that exceeds expectations. Here the lamb is steeped with lemon and artichokes, a traditionally Greek combination that I love. Mint and parsley chopped on top gives a perfectly fresh finish, and my vote would be for a spoonful of polenta, too.

PREP TIME 25 MINUTES   SERVES 4   COOK TIME 2½ HOURS

3 tablespoons olive oil

1kg lean shoulder of lamb, cut into 3cm cubes

1 large onion, roughly chopped

4 garlic cloves, peeled and thinly sliced

2 tablespoons red wine vinegar

300ml red wine

1 tablespoon tomato purée

1 x 400g tin chopped tomatoes

1 x 400g tin/jar artichoke hearts, chargrilled or in brine

Grated zest of 1 lemon and 2 tablespoons lemon juice

1 x 400g tin cannellini beans, drained and rinsed

Sea salt and freshly ground black pepper

Fresh mint and flat-leaf parsley, to garnish

1 Preheat the oven to 170°C/gas mark 3. Heat 2 tablespoons of the olive oil in a deep, ovenproof casserole over a high heat and brown the lamb pieces in batches until each is well coloured. Transfer to a bowl and set aside.

3 Reduce the heat to medium and add the remaining olive oil. Add the onion to the pot and fry for 3–4 minutes until it is tender and soft. Add the garlic for the last couple of minutes. Return the lamb to the pot.

4 Turn the heat up and pour over the vinegar. Cook until it has almost evaporated, then add 200ml of the wine, the tomato purée and chopped tomatoes. Season with pinches of salt and plenty of grinds of black pepper. Cover with a lid and pop in the oven for 1¾ hours.

5 Remove from the oven and stir in the artichokes, lemon zest and juice, cannellini beans and remaining wine (if you think a little more liquid is needed). Return to the oven and cook for a further 30 minutes with no lid.

6 Serve sprinkled liberally with the fresh parsley and mint.

 TIP – TO MAKE POLENTA: BRING 800ML–1 LITRE DELICIOUS CHICKEN STOCK TO THE BOIL IN A MEDIUM-SIZED POT. SLOWLY POUR IN 200G POLENTA AND STIR AS QUICKLY AS YOUR WRISTS ALLOW TO BEAT OUT THE LUMPS. BUBBLE THE POLENTA FOR A FEW MINUTES, STIRRING, UNTIL THICKENED. REMOVE FROM THE HEAT, STIR IN 50G BUTTER AND 50G FINELY GRATED PARMESAN CHEESE. SEASON, SEASON, SEASON AND SERVE. DELICIOUS.

TENDER LAMB MEATBALLS
WITH SWEETCORN & BALSAMIC

In my opinion, meatballs have suffered from school-dinner syndrome and, as a result, have an undeservedly poor reputation, but they can be sophisticated and punchy. Here, I've simply added cumin and fresh herbs to lamb mince and I think it's made all the difference… it's the little things. Serve with rice or chunks of bread.

PREP TIME 15 MINUTES	SERVES 4	COOK TIME 45 MINUTES

500g minced lamb

2 tablespoons roughly chopped flat-leaf parsley

1 teaspoon ground cumin

2–3 tablespoons vegetable oil

FOR THE SAUCE

1 large onion, roughly chopped

3 garlic cloves, peeled and sliced

½ teaspoon cumin seeds

2 x 400g tins chopped tomatoes

2 tablespoons balsamic vinegar

1 tablespoon brown sugar

2 corn on the cob, 1 with the kernels stripped off and
   1 cut into 5–6 equal chunks

2 tablespoons roughly chopped flat-leaf parsley

Sea salt and freshly ground black pepper

1 First off, make the meatballs. Put the mince into a medium-sized bowl with the ground cumin and parsley and use your hands to combine thoroughly. Season. Make 10–12 balls, each about the size of a golf ball.

2 Heat the vegetable oil in a flameproof casserole or deep-sided frying pan and fry the meatballs on all sides, wiggling as you go to brown all over. You may have to do this in batches. When they are ready, remove them from the pan.

3 For the sauce, turn the heat down slightly, add a splash more oil, throw the onion and garlic into the pan and cook until translucent – about 4 minutes. Add the cumin seeds and cook for another couple of minutes.

4 Pour in the chopped tomatoes and either chop up a bit more with a wooden spoon in the pan or just leave them as they are. Add the vinegar and sugar and bring to a simmer.

5 Lower the heat and return the meatballs to the pan. Cook, covered, on a low heat for about 20 minutes. Add the sweetcorn chunks and kernels and simmer for a final 10 minutes without the lid on.

6 Just before serving, check the seasoning and freshen up with some fresh chopped parsley.

MINT & REDCURRANT
LAMB WITH BEANS

We all have people who have been an inspiration to us and mine is Milla. She was the catalyst to my love of cooking, and together we can paw over cookbooks and discuss restaurants late into the night. It was during one such session in Norfolk that we developed this recipe. The redcurrant jelly slowly melts while the fresh mint lightens the lamb. One note before you begin: it may seem like a lot of beans but, trust us, the quantities complement each other.

PREP TIME 20 MINUTES   **SERVES 6**   COOK TIME 2 HOURS

1.7–2kg leg of lamb

4 garlic cloves, peeled but kept whole

1 good sprig of rosemary

2 tablespoons olive oil

2 heaped tablespoons roughly chopped mint

2 x 400g tins flageolet beans, drained and rinsed

125g redcurrant jelly, warmed

400g cherry tomatoes

3–4 large courgettes, halved lengthways and chopped into 1cm crescents

200ml vegetable stock

Sea salt and freshly ground black pepper

1 Preheat the oven to 200°C/gas mark 6.

2 Make incisions all over your lamb by poking the tip of a knife through the skin. Rub the lamb all over with the garlic, then poke halved cloves and rosemary tufts into the incisions as though you're planting cuttings in the garden. Place in a deep roasting tin and drizzle over the olive oil.

3 Roast the lamb in the oven for 1 hour, until it's just starting to turn golden. Meanwhile, combine the chopped mint, beans, redcurrant jelly, cherry tomatoes, sliced courgettes and stock. Season enthusiastically.

4 Remove the lamb from the oven briefly and spoon the bean mixture around the joint until it is surrounded by a sea of beans. Reduce the temperature to 180°C/gas mark 4 and return the joint to the oven for 1 hour or until the lamb is cooked as you wish (a good test is that the meat has pulled away from the bone, leaving the top exposed).

5 Remove the lamb from the beans and allow the meat to rest for 10 minutes before carving. This is the moment when you can add a little more stock to the beans if you think it's needed. Season and spoon onto hot plates with a good hunk of lamb.

 TIP – I LIKE A LITTLE MORE FRESH CHOPPED MINT STIRRED THROUGH THE BEANS JUST BEFORE SERVING.

LAMB TAGINE

Perhaps one of the most distinguished cooking vessels, the traditional African tagine towers majestically over other plain-looking pots. Yet the design is not simply beautiful; it serves a purpose and adds to the dish. You see, steam rises up inside the conical lid and re-condenses before trickling back down the side of the pot and into the stew, keeping it moist and saucy. With water shortages rife in Africa, every little drop is conserved and appreciated. Of course, if you don't happen to have a tagine handy, a sturdy casserole does the job perfectly. Serve this lamb tagine with toasted couscous (see tip below) and a glass of fresh mint tea.

PREP TIME 20 MINUTES   SERVES 6   COOK TIME 2 HOURS

A good glug of olive oil

1.3kg shoulder or leg of lamb, cut into 2.5cm cubes

2 onions, roughly chopped

1 large knob of fresh ginger, peeled and chopped

3 garlic cloves, peeled and each cut into 2

1 cinnamon stick

2 teaspoons ground coriander

1 teaspoon ground cumin

1 teaspoon ground allspice

150g Medjool dates, pitted and roughly chopped if they are large ones

A trickle of runny honey

400g chopped tomatoes

Thinly pared zest of 1 lemon (use a vegetable peeler)

300ml lamb stock

Sea salt and freshly ground black pepper

1 Heat 1 tablespoon olive oil in a 4-litre, heavy-based pot. Season the lamb and cook in batches, on a high heat, until the pieces have begun to brown on all sides. Remove from the pan and set aside.

2 Reduce the heat to low and add a little more oil to the pan if needed. Gently fry the onions, ginger and garlic for 5–10 minutes, until softened. Add the cinnamon stick, ground coriander, cumin and allspice and combine well. Take a moment to breathe in the spell of the spices.

3 Return the browned lamb to the pot, then add the dates, honey, chopped tomatoes, lemon zest and lamb stock. Season and bring to the boil, cover with a lid and cook on a low heat for 1½ hours, by which time the lamb should be beautifully tender. Remove the lid and cook for a further 10 minutes so the juice becomes syrupy.

 TIP – TAGINES ARE DELICIOUS SERVED WITH COUSCOUS. TO MAKE YOUR COUSCOUS ALL THE MORE FLAVOURSOME, DRY-TOAST IT FIRST – SIMPLY PUT A HEAVY-BASED FRYING PAN ON THE HEAT AND ADD THE GRANULES. KEEP TOSSING THEM AROUND THE PAN UNTIL THEY START TO TURN GOLDEN. ADD THE STOCK AND CARRY ON AS USUAL. THE COUSCOUS WILL HAVE DEVELOPED A DISTINCT NUTTY TASTE WHICH GIVES A LITTLE MORE DEPTH.

PERFECT POTS *of* PUDDING

Some of us are just born with a sweet tooth, and some of us aren't. Sadly for my thighs, I fit snugly into the first category and as such need to punctuate every meal with a sweet exclamation mark.

It might also be that in my world puddings often mean an end of meal game. Here's one of my friend Sam's inventions: film tennis, which should last as long as it takes to eat a Muscat jelly. Divide any diners into two teams and decide on a famous film star. Next, and it is this simple, each team takes a turn in naming a film in which this star has played a part. Keep batting the answers back and forth until one team triumphs with better film knowledge!

Please also note that I've deviated with my one pot puddings just a tiny bit. It seems a bit trickier to make puddings in one pot, but they are still simple as can be. And some of the recipes aren't served in one pot - but it's always nice to be given your own portion – it makes it very clear what is yours and there is no chance of anybody doing any stealing.

PEACH, MINT
& BRIOCHE TRIFLE

Trifle strikes me as a festive pudding, a frivolous combination of all things naughty that sits overnight, bonding next to the mince pies and thawing turkey. But here we have a recipe for summer trifle that rivals its Christmas counterpart with fresh ingredients – a hint of sweet and the obligatory dusting of alcohol. Serve with ice-cold Pimms, a rum punch, or even a glass of chilled wine.

PREP TIME 15 MINUTES SERVES 10 CHILL TIME 3 HOURS

6 finger brioche rolls (or 6 slices from a brioche loaf)

100g raspberry jam

100ml sweet wine

500g ready-made vanilla custard

200ml extra thick double cream (or double cream whipped to stiff peaks)

2 tablespoons icing sugar, sifted, plus extra for dusting

2 small ripe peaches, stoned and cut into slices

200g beautiful fresh raspberries

2 tablespoons finely chopped mint, plus an extra sprig of mint or lemon balm leaves to garnish

25g shelled pistachio nuts, roughly chopped

1 Slice the brioche rolls through the middle horizontally and spread half of them with raspberry jam. Sandwich together with their other halves and then cut each mini loaf into lots of 1cm slices. Arrange half of the slices attractively in the base of 10 wine glasses or a 2-litre glass serving dish. Sprinkle the pudding wine over the brioche.

2 In a small bowl, combine the custard and double cream and sweeten with the icing sugar. Drop half of the mixture in spoonfuls over the brioche. Arrange nearly all the peach slices and half of the raspberries over the custard mixture, then dust with a little finely chopped mint.

3 Now you do it all again in a second layer. Start with the brioche slices, then custard mixture and finally the remaining raspberries, peach slices and mint. Finish off with the chopped pistachios.

4 Chill for at least 3 hours and then serve triumphantly dusted with icing sugar and garnished with a sprig of mint or some lemon balm.

PLUM TARTE TATIN

The French have a knack for creating tarts that set the benchmark for puddings, and the classic tarte tatin is no exception. Buying ready-made puff pastry is the cook's bonus – you don't have to be a pastry chef to make this one turn out perfectly.

PREP TIME 25 MINUTES   **SERVES 6**   COOK TIME 30 MINUTES

500g ready-made puff pastry
50g unsalted butter
100g light brown soft sugar
1 vanilla pod, seeds removed (optional)

2 tablespoons Amaretto (optional)
400g firm Victoria plums (enough to cover the base
   of the pan), cut into halves

1 Preheat the oven to 220°C/gas mark 7.

2 Roll out the puff pastry on a lightly floured surface and cut out a 26cm circle. Place in the fridge and chill while you make the rest of the tart.

3 Melt the butter in a 24cm ovenproof frying pan. Add the sugar, vanilla seeds and Amaretto (if using) and melt over a medium/low heat. Shake the pan gently but do not stir, and allow to bubble for a minute.

4 Arrange the plums, cut-side down, on top of the caramel in a spiral pattern. Cover with the prepared pastry circle and tuck the edges inside the pan around the plums.

5 Place in the preheated oven and bake for 30 minutes or until the pastry is golden brown and puffed up. Remove from the oven and leave to cool for 10 minutes before inverting a serving plate over the pan and flipping over as fast as your arms allow. Serve warm with cream.

 TIP – THIS IS A GREAT PUDDING FOR PREPARING IN ADVANCE. MAKE THE WHOLE LOT – I.E. THE CARAMEL WITH PLUMS PATIENTLY SITTING AND THE PUFF PASTRY CIRCLE TUCKED ON TOP – AND LEAVE ASIDE. JUST POP IN THE OVEN 40 MINUTES BEFORE YOU WANT TO SERVE.

MUMMA'S BLUEBERRY
& VANILLA STEAMED SPONGE

Something wonderful happens when a cake mixture is cooked with steam whereby the texture is transformed to a moist honeycomb. I have to hand over the credit for this recipe to my mother who puffs, proud as a peacock, every time this pudding hits the table.

PREP TIME 20 MINUTES · SERVES 6–8 · COOK TIME 2 HOURS

175g softened butter, plus a little extra for greasing

175g caster sugar

Grated zest of 1 lemon

1 teaspoon vanilla extract

3 medium free-range eggs, lightly beaten

100g blueberries

1 tablespoon plain flour

175g self-raising flour

½ teaspoon baking powder

Golden syrup, to serve

1 Grease a 1.2-litre pudding basin liberally with the softened butter.

2 In a medium-sized bowl, cream together the butter and sugar until pale and light. Stir in the lemon zest and vanilla extract, then slowly add the beaten eggs.

3 Lightly wash the blueberries in water, drain off any excess water, then sprinkle the plain flour over the fruit.

4 Fold the self-raising flour and baking powder through the creamed mixture and finally fold through the floury blueberries (the flour on the outside will help them cling to the batter and not all sink to the bottom).

5 Spoon the mixture into the pudding basin and cover with buttered kitchen foil, making a pleat in the foil across the top of the basin. Tie firmly with string.

6 Steam for 2 hours, until risen. If you don't own a steamer, put an upturned saucer in a deep pan (this will act as a trivet) and rest your pudding basin on the top. Add cold water until it's about a quarter of the way up the basin. Put the pan on the heat and bring to the boil. Lower the temperature and keep topping up with water, more often than you think, every 20–25 minutes to make sure there is constant steam.

7 To serve, run a knife round the sides of the bowl, turn out and lavishly smother golden syrup on the top.

TIP - IF YOU UNVEIL YOUR PUDDING AND FEAR THAT IT MAY NOT BE COOKED THROUGH IN THE MIDDLE (PERHAPS A LITTLE WATER HAS TUNNELLED ITS WAY INSIDE), GIVE IT 30 SECONDS ON HIGH IN THE MICROWAVE. NOT THE BEST, I KNOW, BUT WHEN THERE ARE SIX HUNGRY PEOPLE WAITING FOR THEIR PUDDING...

BANANA BREAD
& BUTTER PUDDDING

Some puddings are a throwback to school days and this is certainly one. More often than not the memories of bread and butter pudding need to be banished and erased… and then reinvented. This recipe is a super-speedy version that doesn't require a pre-made custard; it is, as you'd expect, a one-pot version. A rustic crust hides wobbly custard while flecks of fruit offer familiar comfort; all that is needed is a blob of ice cream gently melting by its side.

PREP TIME 15 MINUTES
(PLUS 30 MINUTES SOAKING)

SERVES 6

COOK TIME 40 MINUTES

2 tablespoons softened unsalted butter, plus extra for
    greasing

6 slices of crusty white bread

2 medium free-range eggs

450ml whole milk

30g light brown soft sugar, plus 2 tablespoons extra for
    the crunchy top

1 teaspoon vanilla extract

Grated zest of 1 lemon

2–3 very ripe bananas (nearly brown is just fine),
    cut lengthways into 0.5cm strips

40g juicy raisins (optional)

Cream, to serve

1 Lightly butter a 1-litre ovenproof dish.

2 Butter the bread lightly and cut diagonally in half to form triangles.

3 Crack the eggs into a medium bowl and beat lightly for a minute or so using a hand-held electric whisk. Pour over the milk and continue to beat for another minute. Stir through the sugar, vanilla and lemon zest and whisk to combine.

4 Now there's the arranging. Place the buttered triangles into the dish with the longest side touching the base so they look like mountains. Arrange a triangle of bread at one end, then a banana slither, then bread and so on until you see a mountain range forming. It's easiest to fill both ends of the dish and where both ends meet in the middle, curl the bread and banana to fit the space.

5 Gently pour over the milk mixture, taking care to cover each piece of bread, and allow to sit for 30 minutes. Preheat the oven to 180°C/gas mark 4.

6 Scatter the pudding with raisins (if using) and the extra 2 tablespoons of brown sugar. Fill a roasting tin half way up with water to make a bain-marie and place the pudding in the centre. Bake in the oven for 35–40 minutes. Remove from the oven and allow to sit for a few minutes before serving with ice cold ice cream.

RASPBERRY, ALMOND
& APPLE JUMBLE

Possibly my new favourite dessert. Tart fruit, dense custard and pastry married in their own little pastry pot. Ticks the pudding box very prettily, very prettily indeed.

PREP TIME 15 MINUTES   **SERVES 6**   COOK TIME 30 MINUTES

A little flour, for dusting

500g readymade puff pastry

2 tablespoons custard powder

100g caster sugar

100g ground almonds

1 medium free-range egg

400g Bramley apples (approx. 2), peeled, cored
   and thinly sliced

100g fresh raspberries

1 tablespoon whole milk, for brushing

1 tablespoon dark brown soft sugar

1 tablespoon flaked almonds

Double cream, to serve

1 Preheat the oven to 190°C/gas mark 5.

2 Dust the work surface with a little flour and roll out the puff pastry until it's approximately 0.5cm thick. Cut out a 30cm circle (I'd find a large plate or saucepan lid to trace around with a knife) and slide this onto a baking sheet.

3 In a small bowl, mix your custard powder, 50g of the caster sugar, the ground almonds and egg. Stir until you have a thick paste.

4 Spread the almond paste in the centre of your circle of puff pastry, leaving a good 6cm around the edge. Pile the apple slices and raspberries on top of the paste.

5 Now comes the moment where you create your own pastry pot! Brush the 6cm edge with milk and gather the pastry edge around your fruit pile so you can still see lots of fruit in the centre. Brush the outside of the pastry with a little more milk and pop into the oven.

6 Bake your pie for 20 minutes. Remove from the oven and sprinkle over the brown sugar and flaked almonds. Return to the oven for a further 10 minutes. Serve in slices with a good glug of cold, fresh double cream swimming on the side.

PASSION FRUIT
& LEMON CURD POTS

Such a deliciously simple pudding to put together and a good one for those messy chefs who like flinging ingredients into a bowl. I've used passion fruit, but you can try any fruit that is in season – such as raspberries, strawberries, poached rhubarb or stewed apple and cinnamon – for an equally successful pud.

PREP TIME 15 MINUTES   **SERVES 6**   FREEZING TIME 1 HOUR

200g good-quality lemon curd
Thinly pared zest and juice of 1 large lemon
500ml thickly set Greek yogurt
100g ginger nut biscuits or shortbread, lightly crumbled
 into 1cm pieces

3 passion fruits
25g shelled pistachio buts, roughly chopped

You will also need 6 x 150ml glass tumblers

1 In a small bowl, mix the lemon curd with a little lemon juice so the consistency becomes that of thick treacle. Stir a little water or milk into the Greek yogurt if it's too thick – the consistency should be the same as the lemon mixture.

2 Drop alternate spoonfuls of lemon mixture, Greek yogurt (reserving a little for the top), crushed ginger nut biscuits and passion fruit pulp into each of the 6 tumblers.

Don't worry about being too neat; this is a jumbled dessert, which improves if it's a bit messy.

3 Top with a blob of the reserved yogurt, chopped pistachios and a swirl of lemon zest then freeze for just 1 hour: don't let the yogurt become too solid. Serve with a silver teaspoon.

TIP – IF YOU HAVE MADE THESE IN ADVANCE, ALLOW THE PUDDINGS TO 'COME TO' IN A COOL AREA (NO NEED TO REFRIGERATE) FOR 2 HOURS OR SO BEFORE SERVING. IT WILL MAKE THEM EASIER TO ATTACK. .

MUSCAT, CHERRY
& APPLE JELLY

A most delicate and pretty dessert that captures fruit in crystal-clear suspension and suggests cooking prowess by any host who is able to deliver. One word of warning: many cooks get nervous at the gelatine moment, tossing up whether to add more than the instructions suggest, 'just to be safe'. My advice? Don't do it; a soft-set jelly trumps any bouncy-ball equivalent and the instructions are generally right.

PREP TIME 20 MINUTES   SERVES 4   SETTING TIME 4–5 HOURS

4 leaves of gelatine (enough to set approx. 525ml)

37.5cl Muscat (or any other pudding wine)

1 tablespoon caster sugar

150ml fizzy water

150g cherries, pitted, plus 4 extra to decorate

½ small green apple, cored and thinly sliced

You will also need 4 x 250ml stemmed glasses

1 Soak the gelatine in cold water for 5 minutes or so. The texture of the leaves will change from that of solid glass window panes to pliable, see-through jelly. Remove from the liquid and squeeze with your hands to remove as much liquid as possible.

2 Pour the Muscat into a pan and heat gently, not allowing it to simmer. Remove from the heat and add the sugar. Stir until it has dissolved and add the softened gelatine leaves until they have all but disappeared. Stir through the fizzy water.

3 Allow the mixture to cool slightly (about 10 minutes) – this will help the fruit to be suspended in your glasses rather than just float to the top.

4 Place a dense cluster of cherries and apple at the base of each of your glasses and gently pour over a few centimetres of liquid. As the fruit begins to float, stop and place the glasses in the fridge.

5 After about 1 hour, when the fruit will no longer bob to the surface, pour the remaining jelly over the fruit. Allow to set for 3–4 hours. Serve.

POMEGRANATE
& PISTACHIO RICE PUDDING

It always surprises me that tiny grains of pudding rice drink far more than their body weight in creamy milk. The quantities seem unlikely when you first put them in the pan, but with love and persistence all that liquid is soaked up. You're left with the most beautiful of puddings – a snowy-white mountain, kissed with molasses and the greens and reds of pistachios and pomegranates.

PREP TIME 10 MINUTES   SERVES 4   COOK TIME 45 MINUTES

100g short-grain pudding rice, rinsed under cold
   running water
75g caster sugar
Grated zest of 2 lemons

800ml –1 litre whole milk
2 tablespoons pomegranate molasses
2 tablespoons fresh pomegranate seeds
25g shelled pistachio nuts, roughly chopped

1 Place the rice, sugar, lemon zest and milk in a saucepan. Bring to the boil over a medium heat, stirring occasionally. Reduce the heat and simmer, stirring frequently, for 35 minutes or until the rice is soft and swollen and the milk is absorbed. Add a little more milk if you think it's needed, as everyone's pudding will boil at a slightly different pace.

2 Serve immediately, drizzled with tart pomegranate molasses, the pomegranate seeds and green pistachios.

MAPLE-BAKED OATS
WITH FIGS

Ideally, brunch suggests lazy mornings spent lazing in pyjamas with lazy food that doesn't require too much tending. Here, you'll find a cross between a warming porridge and a flapjack, with beautiful figs and delicate tart apple running through the oats. Common to most brunches, syrup is an absolute must! A brunch without maple is like a Mountie without his hat.

PREP TIME 10 MINUTES   SERVES 6   COOK TIME 35–40 MINUTES

500ml semi-skimmed milk

2 medium free-range eggs

30g unsalted butter, melted

75ml maple syrup

4 tablespoons dark brown soft sugar

1 large cooking apple, peeled, cored and cut into
    1cm cubes

4 –5 ripe figs, each cut into 8

200g rolled oats

1 heaped teaspoon baking powder

1 teaspoon ground allspice

A pinch of salt

50g flaked almonds

Yogurt, to serve

1 Preheat the oven to 180°C/gas mark 4. Grease the bottom of a 1-litre dish.

2 In a small bowl or jug, gently whisk the milk, eggs, melted butter, maple syrup and half the sugar.

3 Tumble the chunks of apple and half the figs into your dish with the oats, baking powder, allspice and salt. Give everything a good jumble around using your hands or a large spoon. Gently pour over the milk mixture and allow it to soak in for a few minutes.

4 Sprinkle the remaining figs, the flaked almonds and the remaining sugar onto the mixture, then bake in the oven for 35–40 minutes until the milk has become fully absorbed. Serve while still warm with yogurt for a delicious brunch dish.

3-MINUTE CHOCOLATE
MUG CAKE

Imagine the things you could do in three minutes: make a cup of tea, brush your teeth, listen to a Beatles song, make the bed, do a Sudoku, write a (probably not very good) haiku... And make a cake! Welcome to the world of microwave chocolate mug cake. I take no responsibility for the recipe, nor can I say that the result is the most complex, interesting cake; but nonetheless it definitely fills a hole.

PREP TIME 2 MINUTES · SERVES 2 · COOK TIME 3 MINUTES

4 tablespoons plain flour

4 tablespoons caster sugar

2 tablespoons cocoa powder

1 medium free-range egg

3 tablespoons semi-skimmed milk

3 tablespoons vegetable oil

A small splash of vanilla or orange extract

Grated zest of 1 large orange

1 Put the dry ingredients in a bowl and mix well. Add the egg, stir, then pour in the milk and oil. Mix well again.

2 Add the vanilla/orange extract and orange zest and mix. Pour into 2 large mugs and cook in the microwave for 3 minutes at 1000 watts.

3 The cake might rise over the top of the mugs, but don't be afraid – the mixture will set. Allow to cool a little, then tip out onto plates and serve each cake with a good spoonful of good-quality ice cream.

SEXY COFFEE
& HAZELNUT POTS

There is a reason why these tiny pots are but two or three mouthfuls – you couldn't, or at least shouldn't, eat too much more. Your thighs wouldn't thank you.

PREP TIME 10 MINUTES   SERVES 8   COOK TIME 15 MINUTES

170g caster sugar
75g cocoa powder
50g plain flour
2 medium free-range eggs
500ml semi-skimmed milk

1 teaspoon instant coffee granules
A handful of hazelnuts, skin on

You will need 8 x 100ml pots

1 Weigh the sugar, cocoa powder and plain flour into a large saucepan and make a well in the centre.

2 Crack your eggs into the well and stir, gradually incorporating the dry ingredients to form a chocolatey paste. Slowly add the milk and beat with a wooden spoon until all is added. Stir though the coffee.

3 Place the saucepan on a low heat (don't be tempted to increase the heat or the eggs will cook too quickly and you will be left with scrambled eggs) and continue to stir for about 15 minutes, until the mixture has thickened and is beginning to form small lumps on the spoon. The consistency should be that of extra thick double cream.

4 Remove from the heat and, using a hand whisk, beat out the lumps with enthusiastic vigour; they will disappear.

5 Divide the mixture between 8 pots or cups and scatter over the hazelnuts. Allow to set for a couple of hours before serving.

INDEX